Sissinghurst

The Elizabethan tower which dominates Sissinghurst seen from the Cottage Garden.

Sissinghurst
The Making of a Garden

ANNE SCOTT-JAMES

London
MICHAEL JOSEPH

First published in Great Britain by Michael Joseph Ltd
44 Bedford Square, London WC1
FEBRUARY 1975
SECOND IMPRESSION JUNE 1975
THIRD IMPRESSION NOVEMBER 1975
FOURTH IMPRESSION JULY 1978
FIFTH IMPRESSION JANUARY 1981
SIXTH IMPRESSION MARCH 1983

ISBN 0 7181 1278 4 (cased edition)
ISBN 0 7181 2256 9 (paperback edition)

Filmset in eleven on thirteen point Baskerville
by Filmtype Services, Scarborough
Printed in Great Britain by Redwood Burn Limited
Trowbridge, Wiltshire and bound by
Dorstel Press Ltd, Harlow

To Clare

Contents

Illustrations

COLOUR PLATES

BLACK AND WHITE

Foreword

In a long career as a writer I have always (not unnaturally)
had to do my own thinking, clawing my ideas out of the air.
Then, in the spring of 1973, a plum dropped into my lap.
Mrs. Michael Joseph asked if I would write the history of the
garden of Sissinghurst. She had the authority of Mr. Nigel
Nicolson to put the proposal, who had inherited Sissinghurst
from his mother, V. Sackville-West. In 1967, he transferred
the castle and garden to the National Trust, but he lives
there still, as may his family in perpetuity, and works closely
with the Trust to preserve Sissinghurst's extraordinary
beauty. Though aware of the responsibility, I accepted the
offer at once and caught a train to Kent the next day.

The task has been pure pleasure. I have spent many days
in one of the loveliest gardens in the world and many evenings
studying the documents to which Mr. Nicolson gave me full
access – diaries, letters both published and unpublished,
garden notebooks, albums of photographs, and, most generously, his own abundant notes and memoirs. I am profoundly
grateful for his help and hospitality.

Many others at Sissinghurst helped me, most notably the
head gardeners, Miss Pamela Schwerdt and Miss Sibylle
Kreutzberger, who, faced with my ignorance of many of the

rarer plants of Sissinghurst, were patience itself. They not only checked my manuscript but worked with me on the drafting of the last three chapters on the garden of Sissinghurst today, which could never have been written without their expert knowledge. I must also thank officials of the National Trust for the time they have spared me and the detailed information they have collated for me; and many friends of the late Sir Harold Nicolson and his wife, V. Sackville-West, the creators of the garden, for their recollections, especially Miss Ursula Codrington, who was Miss Sackville-West's secretary for the last three years of her life.

Alas, I never knew either Harold Nicolson or his wife, but after first introducing them by their full names I have referred to them as Harold and Vita for simplicity's sake.

I must say a word about nomenclature. Since I am an amateur gardening writer, not a botanist, I felt that strict botanical spelling would be an affectation, and further, the repeated use of single inverted commas is typographically exhausting to the eye; so I have put all Latin plant names in italics and all English, French or other modern names in Roman type.

Since words alone can never recreate a work of art, I have used as many illustrations as printing costs allow. I believe that no garden photographer ever went to Sissinghurst once only – its beauty always draws them back again and again.

Acknowledgements. I am indebted to Mr. Nigel Nicolson for permission to print the poem *Sissinghurst*, by V. Sackville-West, as well as many extracts from *The Land* and *The Garden*; and for permission to quote from two broadcasts by Harold Nicolson from his book of collected broadcasts, *People and Things*. I must particularly thank Miss Pamela Schwerdt for the colour photographs which appear facing pages 48, 64, 65, 112, 113, 128, 129 and the photograph of The Bishops' Gate facing page 49, which have not been published before. The colour photograph taken inside the White Garden facing page 49 is by Leonard Gayton. The photograph of the Nicolsons on the tower steps facing page 33 is by Philip Turner, and the black-and-white photographs facing pages 80, 81, 96, 97 and the photograph of Vita's writing table facing page 33 are by Edwin Smith.

1

From the Top
of the Tower

The visitor to Sissinghurst Castle who knows the garden well
derives his pleasure from strolling erratically from one well-
loved enclosure to another, enjoying the plants which billow
from every corner and the shafts of scent which assail him as
he goes. But the visitor who sees Sissinghurst for the first time
would be wise to start his tour by climbing to the top of the
soaring Elizabethan tower. From this vantage point, two
qualities become clear which are essential to an understand-
ing of the garden – its close-knit relationship with the
surrounding country and its severity of design.

Sissinghurst is a true country garden. The view from the
top of the tower is wholly rural, with the patchwork fields of
the Kentish weald stretching as far as the eye can see. There
is a dark fringe of woods to the south and single ancient oak-
trees, which look dumpy from this height, are dotted about
the landscape. Two towers of village churches pierce the
horizon on a clear day, that of Frittenden to the north and
Biddenden in the east. The approach to the castle is by a
winding country lane and the buildings of Sissinghurst
Castle Farm cluster round the castle entrance. Just outside
the gatehouse are the farmhouse itself, a robust Victorian
building with handsome chimneys, a group of oasthouses,

15

an Elizabethan barn and white weatherboarded granaries, and the scene is usually bustling with men on tractors and herds of cows in the fields. The men are really working and the cows are really munching, for the farm is a thriving business, not an essay in the picturesque. Sissinghurst has no lodge, no sweeping drive, no imposing gates. It is a jumble of mellow brick buildings with mossy roofs set in the middle of fields, friendly and unpretentious, more of a manor house than a castle.

When he has seen the countrified nature of the site, the visitor will more readily appreciate the planting of the garden. This will be discussed in detail later in this book; it is only necessary now to notice how harmonious it is with its surroundings, the garden melting easily into the open country, with avenues of poplars to link the two together. The weald of Kent is abundant and fertile, and so is the garden, green with velvety grass and richly crowded with plants, with many Kentish specialities such as apple-trees, a nuttery and hedges of indigenous hornbeam and yew. The castle architecture is romantic and wayward and again, the planting is in tune. Plants are mixed with joyous informality and allowed freedom to grow naturally with a minimum use of stakes, secateurs and shears. All the plants, whether hardy or tender, are appropriate to the local soil. Many are of a wild or cottagey nature, and there are hundreds of old-fashioned plants and plant species, quite ordinary plants rubbing shoulders with botanical rarities.

The second quality of the garden best seen from the tower is its design, which is a brilliant solution of an extraordinarily complex problem.

Sissinghurst garden was made by two people, the late Sir Harold Nicolson and his wife, Vita Sackville-West. He was the designer and she the plantsman and they worked in perfect harmony. He liked rational, classical things and she liked the poetic and romantic, but fortunately, their conception of an ideal garden was a fusion of the two. They wanted a strict, formal design with free, informal planting. They also wanted a garden of a private, almost secret nature.

ABOVE
Vita with her sons, Ben and
Nigel, at Long Barn in 1929.
Here she and Harold made a
garden which was the forerunner
of Sissinghurst.

RIGHT
Steps thick with flowers led
down from Vita's sitting-room at
Long Barn.

Sissinghurst in 1930, a junkyard of weeds and rubbish. The arch was unblocked in 1931.

The South Cottage seen from the top of the tower in 1930. On the right is the site of the future Cottage Garden and Lime Walk.

The visitor with the bird's-eye view can see both the formality and the privacy of the design – and the great talent needed to achieve it. For Sissinghurst did not lend itself readily to a formal plan. One feels that Le Nôtre, the designer of the geometrically perfect park of Versailles, would have been disgusted with it.

The site is a rectangle, but a rough one, bounded on two sides by a moat, and inside the rectangle the castle buildings are all askew. The tower is not parallel with the entrance buildings, so that the first courtyard is not a true rectangle, the space between the Moat Walk and the nuttery is an odd coffin shape, and, as V. Sackville-West herself wrote, there are many "minor crookednesses". All these were skilfully camouflaged by Harold Nicolson to make a formal garden patterned with straight axes leading to focal points. The curious geometry visible from the tower seems deliberate and orderly on the ground.

The sense of privacy that both husband and wife wanted was achieved by dividing the garden into many separate enclosures opening off the main walks, each surrounded by walls or by high, architectural hedges. Each enclosure is formal in shape, planted with romantic freedom. The Front Court, the Tower Lawn, the White Garden, the Rose Garden, the Rondel, the Lime Walk (or Spring Garden), the Moat Walk, the Nuttery, the Cottage Garden, the Orchard and the Herb Garden can all be seen, or at least glimpsed, from the tower. How all the enclosures were made, and in what order, and with what pleasures and pains in the making, will be told later on.

Since both the Nicolsons were indefatigable diarists and recorders of plans, dates, anecdotes and impressions, the history of the garden is well documented, but there is one quality which no writer can describe or analyse. The visitor must sense its magic for himself.

2

Apprenticeship

Few people grow passionate about gardening until they have a garden of their own. One can love pictures without owning them or architecture though one lives in a soulless flat, and many devoted music-lovers cannot play a note. But gardening is a craft as well as a form of artistic expression, and to be truly involved in it one must be a practitioner. Living as a mere spectator in a house with a fine garden is not enough; one must have a share in the designing, choose plant material, handle plants and tools and watch one's labours grow, and only then is one a gardener.

This was the case with both Harold Nicolson and Vita Sackville-West. Both were patricians born to life in the grand manner, but Harold, the son of the diplomatist Sir Arthur Nicolson (later Lord Carnock), and nephew of Lord Dufferin, Viceroy of India, was shuttled in his youth from one capital city to another (among them Teheran, where he was born, Constantinople, Sofia, Tangier, Madrid and St. Petersburg), and though interested in architecture at an early stage of his life the thought that he would one day pore over shrub catalogues and plant rare fritillaries never crossed his mind.

Vita might have been expected to have learned the charms of gardening earlier, but this did not happen. The only child

of Lionel and Victoria Sackville-West,* she was born, and
lived until her marriage, at the ancestral home of the Sackvilles, Knole, a great Tudor palace in Kent with three
hundred and sixty five rooms built round seven courtyards,
which she loved literally to distraction; she could never
accept, even in middle age, that as a female she could not
inherit it, and her bitterness never abated.

She loved the great house and the serene walled garden
round it and the glorious 1000-acre park beyond the garden,
and the life of the Kentish countryside where there were trees
to climb, birds' eggs to throw at the servants who came to
look for her when she hid in the woods, and horses to ride,
and her own bicycle. She loved the stags which occasionally
strayed into the banqueting hall** and the dogs she took on
secret coursing expeditions and her pet rabbits, but as yet
she took no particular pleasure in flowers.

There was no gardening talent in her ancestry and the
garden at Knole, which was formal, extending into woodland, had nothing much in the way of a flower garden except
for a conventional herbaceous border. As is the case with most
very large English houses, the lawns sweep right up to the
house, for architecture on a grand scale dwarfs all plants
except trees and provides little scope for the flower gardener.
In any case, there was an army of gardeners at Knole when
Vita was young and the daughter of the house would hardly
have been welcomed as an extra hand. Indeed, she was
terrified of the head gardener, who used to accuse her of
stealing peaches and flowers. "In her deep stagnant gaze
there was no dawning Wanderlust" wrote Violet Trefusis in
her memoirs of Vita at the age of twelve, and in her deep
stagnant gaze there was no dawning flower-lust, either. These
passions came later. However, her mother's diary records
that Vita grew salads and vegetables in a child's corner for
her grandfather and made a large V in cress on a piece of
flannel. And years later, in 1950, she wrote to her uncle, the
4th Lord Sackville, asking if she might have a key of the

---

* Her father became the 3rd Lord Sackville in 1908.
** *See Knole and the Sackvilles*, by V. Sackville-West (1922).

garden gate at Knole in case she ever wished to visit it in secret, so that among her loving memories of Knole the garden had its place.

As soon as she had a garden of her own, plants began to weave their spells on her, and her first garden was in Constantinople. Harold and Vita were married in the chapel at Knole on October 1st, 1913, when she was twenty-one and he five years older, and they went off four days later for a honeymoon in Italy and Egypt from which they went on to Constantinople, where Harold was Third Secretary at the British Embassy. On November 7th, they bought a house in the district of Cospoli, overlooking St. Sophia and the Golden Horn, which Vita described in a letter to a friend as "the most attractive house you have ever seen. It is a wooden Turkish house, with a little garden and a pergola of grapes, and a pomegranate tree covered with scarlet fruit, and such a view over the Golden Horn and the sea and S. Sophia. And on the side of a hill, a perfect suntrap. I find Constantinople lovely." One notes with awe that there were seven servants including a 12-year-old negro boy; all through the Nicolsons' married life, in spite of occasional financial doldrums, there was never a lack of staff; and though Vita, in letters and poems, gives the impression that the house at Cospoli was small, the Ambassador, Sir Louis Mallett, described it as "a large house with many shuttered windows". Vita, coming fresh from Knole, was still thinking on a lordly scale.

The garden at Cospoli had been much neglected – the Nicolsons created three gardens in their lives, at Cospoli, Long Barn and Sissinghurst, and in each case they started with a wilderness – but it was far from bare. There were broken-down wells and fountains and a romantic profusion of old fruit-trees, vines, roses and lilacs, and Vita began at once to restore the garden and to experiment with flowers, and Harold worked with her.

This first garden was not destined to be theirs for long. In the spring of 1914 Harold was recalled to London and they had to pack up and go home, but they brought with them from Cospoli two treasures which were to be mementoes for life, the Greek plaque now on the wall just outside the White Garden and the bowl of very fine marble which is the centre-piece of the Herb Garden at Sissinghurst. It rests on three lions.

Arriving back in England in June, they went to Knole and in August their first son, Ben, was born there two days after the outbreak of war. They did not stay long at Knole because relations with Vita's mother, who was half-Spanish, charming but changeable, by turns affectionate and quarrelsome, became too strained. They bought a house in London in Ebury Street and started looking for a second home in the country. In the spring of 1915 they bought Long Barn, near Sevenoaks, only two miles from magnetic Knole, and this was their home for the next fifteen years.

Long Barn was a 14th century cottage where local pride alleges that Caxton was born, though there is not a shred of evidence to prove it. The cottage had a sound roof but was otherwise in groggy shape, with shaky beams, uneven floors and whole rooms slipping sideways. Mounds of rubble surrounded the house and the garden, which sloped steeply away from the house downhill, consisted of rubbish, rank weeds and a rough field with an old barn at the bottom. This was just the sort of garden of shreds and tatters that the Nicolsons liked, preferring the challenge of creation to the ease of stepping into an estate agent's dream property, and at Long Barn they flexed their muscles, as it were, for Sissinghurst. The gardening interest born at Cospoli grew into a passion and they developed the partnership which was later to prove triumphant on a grander scale.

In this partnership, Harold was the strategist, Vita the tactician. At Long Barn, Harold, who was a descendant of Robert Adam and proud of it, took over the architectural improvements to the house and the designing of the garden and Vita the planting, though she consulted him at every step. It cannot be said too early or too forcibly that Harold was always the garden designer. Although Vita herself wrote repeatedly in essays and articles that Harold was "the ideal collaborator . . . he should have been a garden-architect in another life . . . he has a natural taste for symmetry, and an ingenuity in forcing focal points or long distance views, where everything seemed against him, a capacity I totally lacked'', yet his importance as her co-gardener has never been generally appreciated. The writer feels that there ought to be an addition to the plaque on the tower at Sissinghurst designed by Reynolds Stone, which Harold put up in memory of "Vita Sackville-West who made this garden". She, who was never greedy for credit, would want his name to be engraved there too.

The architectural improvements at Long Barn were entirely successful. The old house was restored and the decrepit barn pulled down and its timbers used to make a handsome new wing, which provided a large ground floor drawing-room with timbered ceilings, oak doors and leaded windows, and guest rooms and bathrooms above. A separate cottage alongside Long Barn luckily fell vacant soon after the Nicolsons moved in and this was bought as well to house the children (a younger son, Nigel, was born three years after Ben). Vita had her own sitting-room – low, timbered, private – in the main house and Harold's study was at the opposite end of the house. Thus the eccentric pattern of family life later followed at Sissinghurst was initiated at Long Barn, the family living in separate quarters and uniting for meals or, when the children were small, for a sociable half-hour with their parents after tea. At first, Harold and Vita lived in London and used Long Barn as a weekend home, but Vita increasingly spent the summer months there, and in 1925, when Harold was posted to Teheran, the London house was sold and she moved to Long Barn altogether.

At Long Barn, unlike Sissinghurst, there were frequent house-parties; the intelligentsia came for weekends – Clive Bell, Virginia Woolf, Raymond Mortimer, Roy Campbell, Gladwyn Jebb, and politicians too, like Venizelos. The food was good, there were plenty of servants, the company was convivial, and there was the grander social life of Knole to mingle with only two miles away. It was an élite society.

While the house was being altered, Harold and Vita began to make the garden which, sloping steeply, had to be entirely terraced. They had two gardeners (Lady Sackville, who was extremely rich, paid for one) and skilled labour and good materials were plentiful and cheap. Quite quickly, the rubbish was cleared away, a terrace was built round the house, semi-circular steps were made leading down to a lawn, retaining walls were constructed to support the terraces, and there was even a tennis court, a social amenity unthinkable at Sissinghurst, restored at a period when the fun was over and Vita had retired into her shell. Their schemes were elaborate and ambitious and in 1917 they bought the neighbouring farm, Brook Farm, which was later to be the inspiration of Vita's long pastoral poem *The Land*.*

With every year at Long Barn, their gardening skill and knowledge grew. A notebook entitled Garden, Long Barn, 1916, shows how little Vita knew in early years, how untutored she was as to plants. On the first page she had scribbled "when and how to plant lilac? When wild thyme? Wild sedums? Little saxifrages? What other good rock things, bushy? Good climbing roses?" The most elementary knowledge was lacking. In the early entries spelling mistakes were plentiful; we read of wichariana ramblers and acquilegia, and in her early lists few specific names are used. She, who later learned to love botanical names, wrote baldly of spirea (pink); monkshood, 4 foot, blue; coreopsis, yellow; orange nemesia.

In the following ten years Vita learned a great deal about plants, and Harold continued to shape the garden making his own surveys and working drawings. They knew from the beginning the kind of garden they wanted. There were to be long, straight vistas and a certain formality and the pattern

---

* *The Land*, published in 1926, won the Hawthornden prize in 1927. It was a celebration of the landscape and the farms, the crops and the flowers, the country people and the rustic pursuits, of Vita's beloved county, Kent.
"The Weald of Kent, once Forest and today
Meadow and orchard, garden of fruit and hops,
A green wet country on a bed of clay."

of terraces was to be intricate. The many low retaining walls were to be clothed with rock plants like aubrieta and helianthemum and the planting of the beds was to be crowded, as in a traditional cottage garden. There were to be many roses and irises, many bulbs, tree lupins and flowering shrubs. Long Barn is on such a different site from Sissinghurst, the one on a hillside, the other flat, that resemblances are hard to trace, but there were, as at Sissinghurst, long grass walks, a hornbeam hedge, rows of Irish yews and an avenue of poplars, and in both cases the walls were thickly latticed with climbers.

There are also primitive signs of the Sissinghurst philosophy of cutting up a garden into "separate rooms". In the course of time, they made a box garden, an enclosure for lilies and roses and a yellow-and-white garden, and Harold had a plan for a series of "little colour gardens in rectangles with nuts and trees and things", meaning a different colour for each enclosure. There was an apple garden and a nuttery, and at the bottom of the slope a Dutch garden was designed for them in 1925 by their great friend "McNed", Sir Edwin Lutyens, but it does not seem to have been his finest hour. However, the house and garden have changed hands so many times since the Nicolsons left that it is difficult to judge the merits of the Dutch garden from the six raised L-shaped beds which are to be seen today.

From the beginning, the Nicolsons were surprisingly well-organized gardeners. They made careful lists of a) things to do and b) things to order, and the things got ordered and done. Their garden was a planned creation, not a haphazard growth, but it was not, like a French garden, a static conception which could be planned, planted and left for ever. They thought of a garden as organic, always growing and changing, and up to the year when they left they were moving nut-trees, planting poplars near the pond, planning new gates and gaps, and ordering innumerable plants. To them, the element of experiment was part of the fun.

Their gardening relationship at Long Barn remained close during all the years they were there, with only one rupture. This was when Vita, as is now well known,* had a passionate love affair with a woman friend, Violet Trefusis, and ran away with her on various occasions to Cornwall, France and Italy. The love affair lasted for three years, from 1918 to 1921, and some of Vita's absences were prolonged into months. As Harold was not only extremely busy with his Foreign Office work, which took him frequently abroad, but also pursued Vita to France, the garden must have been left at this period in the hands of the gardeners. One assumes that they knew their stuff.

When the crisis was over, Vita returned to Long Barn, which she had never ceased to love, and the garden partnership again became important to both. When Harold was away, in London or abroad, he was kept in touch with every detail of the garden news. In 1925 he was posted to Teheran as Counsellor to the British Legation, and Vita, who had no taste for the social chores of a diplomatic hostess, decided to stay in England, but this was no barrier to their collaboration; for the Nicolsons, like many of their Bloomsbury friends, were indefatigable correspondents and wrote to each other every single day. The Foreign Office bag groaned under the weight of their letters going to and fro discussing life, politics, people, the children – and the garden. Many of these letters contained urgent discussion of its progress. Some even contained flowers, for Vita would enclose the petals of some precious bloom which, travelling before the days of Air Mail, cannot have arrived in mint condition.

Throughout the twenties, Harold seems to have been the senior partner, and sent home from Teheran not only many suggestions and sketches but quite brisk reprimands.

In June, 1926, he wrote from Persia that he was "disappointed that the ground is too wet for yews", and suggested instead "a *formal* planting of other trees, either 1) a quincunx of poplars or 2) formal beds and no trees" and added tartly "The one thing you can't do is to leave a few specimen trees. If you do that I shall order it or them to be removed when

* The full story is told in *Portrait of a Marriage*, by Nigel Nicolson.

I get back . . . Don't do anything without my agreeing.''
He sent right-and-wrong sketches of what he had in mind.

A few weeks later, Vita sent him a full plan and description
of a new planting. She has made a path with stepping-stones,
stream and marsh plants and azaleas. She is becoming ever
more enthusiastic. "About the garden, I mind with a flaming
red passion." Luckily, Barnes, the gardener, is proving a
treasure. Harold too, is homesick for Long Barn. "I think
such heaps of the garden. What an enormous part those tilted
acres play in our life!"

In December, 1926, he again wrote to her in admonitory
vein. "Darling, I don't like rhododendrons – I am sorry.
I don't mind them in a big place round a lake. But I think
they are as out of place at the cottage as a billiard-table would
be. To me it is exactly the same. Then I don't like putting in
big things – (as distinct from small flowers) – which are not
indigenous; I am opposed to specimen trees." He suggested
cob-nuts for the space for which she had proposed rhododendrons, with holly as a background. He wanted the garden to
blend with the Kentish scene. Nothing was to be obviously
exotic. He had already evolved a gardening philosophy
extending beyond mere design into the field of planting.

By the mid nineteen-twenties, Vita had learned a great
deal about plants. Her later notes are sophisticated in comparison with the crude lists of 1916. Long lists of irises, tulips
and other bulbs are ordered from different growers to get the
varieties she wants.

Already her love of wild flowers in the garden, so marked
at Sissinghurst, was bearing fruit at Long Barn. She plans
for "wild honeysuckle and dog roses along all the hedges.
Wild cherry in the copse. Pink and red thorn."

In 1926 and 1927, she made two journeys to Persia, where
Harold was *en poste* at Teheran, which fed this love of wild
flowers. Both journeys were adventurous and rewarding;
Persia was the greatest of her travel experiences and she
wrote later that "going to Persia enriched all my life". On
the first journey she went to Teheran alone, travelling over-
land by way of Baghdad and home by way of Russia, and

loved the rocky wildness of the landscape and the sense of space. On the second, she, Harold, Gladwyn Jebb and another friend followed the migration route of the Bakhtiari tribe across a mountain range in the south-east, the wildest part of Persia, travelling by mule and camping at night. On both journeys she was overwhelmed by the beauty of the wild flowers. In a book about the first journey, *Passenger to Teheran*, (published 1926) she notes little grape hyacinths, hillsides full of "sage and the wild lavender with the big pink flower", and wild tulips, "the white ones that are so sweet-scented, and the yellow ones that have no scent at all, but are of a beautiful pure buttercup yellow, like a pointed goblet designed by some early draughtsman with a right instinct for line." She writes of the desert "where the tiny poppies, red and purple, and the tiny scarlet ranunculus grow", finds the native *Iris persica* growing "usually in couples, like marriage, one greenish-white, and one bluish-white, a few yards apart", and yellow scented squills everywhere.

There are also wild almond and many shrubby things, but they interest her less, as she explains with a penetrating comment. "I like my flowers small and delicate – the taste of all gardeners, as their discrimination increases, dwindles towards the microscopic." It would make an excellent discussion subject for a gardening symposium.

The small flowers attract her again on her second adventure, in the Bakhtiari country, described in what is arguably the best of all her books, *Twelve Days* (published 1928). Here "the love of Persia filled my heart again, at the sight of her high solitudes in the purity of an April day", and as before, the flowers were one of the enchantments. "The hills were blue with grape hyacinths", though scentless and not of good colour, and she found a brilliant scarlet ranunculus and a few mauve crocuses. On one occasion the party scattered for a day, and Gladwyn Jebb went off exploring on his own. Great was the chagrin of the Nicolsons when he met them at camp in the evening proudly bearing a bunch of Crown Imperials. A few days later they too found a gorge filled with

Fritillaria imperialis, many, she notes, coming up blind as they are apt to do in English gardens, and on others of the "twelve days" they found gladiolus, anemones, orchises, borage, eremurus, and at last the little scarlet tulip which she had searched for in vain on her first visit. "There it was, blood-red in the sun, and I took the bulbs, and stuck the flowers into the harness of the patient Mouse [her mule]."

It has often been suggested that Sissinghurst shows signs of Persian influence, but this is far-fetched. In the design there is no relationship at all, a Persian garden being rigid and unimaginative in form, while both Sissinghurst and Long Barn are essentially gardens of surprise. The classic conception of a Persian garden, to which all Persian gardens conform, is of a walled enclosure with straight avenues of trees cut by intersecting paths and straight canals of water sometimes running over blue tiles. There is usually a pavilion at the end of the main walk, faced and honeycombed with coloured tiles, and the canals may widen into geometric pools, rectangular, square, octagonal or clover-leaved in shape. The trees are fine and varied – poplars, cypresses, Oriental planes and many others – and there may be almonds and a variety of fruit trees, but few flowers.

Harold positively disliked Persian gardens and wrote scathingly about them while Vita, though "netted in the love of Persia", was sensible enough to see that in that hot, dry country the essentials of a garden are just shady trees and running water. Nothing could be more different from the requirements of the English scene. In any case, very few of the old Persian gardens remain, for they have not been lovingly preserved by the modern Iranians, as the present author has seen for herself. Most have been built over or have lapsed into decay and the flowers which Vita enjoyed in the few tumble-down gardens she managed to find were not cultivated flowers, but desert escapes, such as wild grape hyacinths and tulips. The old poets of Persia, Omar Khayam, Hafiz and Saady, wrote lyrically about flowers, especially roses, but Vita pointed out in an essay on Persian gardens*

* A fine essay published in *Legacy of Persia* in 1927, romantic and appreciative in approach, but far from dewy-eyed.

that there is no word for rose in the Persian language, the only description being "red flower". She found little pleasure in the roses cultivated today and recorded that "in the gardens are poor, stunted tea-roses, but it is for the exuberance of the native wildling that one must wait before one understands the reputation of Persian roses. Huge bushes, compact, not straggling like the English dog-rose, spattered with flame-coloured blossom . . . of a pristine simplicity which our whorled hybrids, superlative though they can be, can never excel."

Vita Sackville-West was not the only writer to notice a disparity between the ancient poetry and art of Persia and the modern reality. Robert Byron describes in *The Road to Oxiana* how he spent frustrating months in the winter of 1933–34 trying to find any appreciation of beauty among the Persians. "Impossible, one thinks, for this swarm of seedy mongrels to be really the race that have endeared themselves to countless travellers with their manners, gardens, horsemanship, and love of literature"; and "one pollarded tree-stump, an empty pond, and a line of washing all dripping with rain, give a new idea of a Persian garden. At the end stood a vaulted summer-house, but just as I put pencil to it, the whole thing collapsed in a heap." Then, one day he was rewarded. He entered the Governor's house in Firuzabad, south of Shiraz, to find this scene. "A tall brass lamp stood between two pewter bowls, one filled with branches of pink fruit blossom, the other with a posy of big yellow jonquils wrapped round a bunch of violets. By the jonquils sat the Governor, with his legs crossed and his hands folded in his sleeves; by the blossom his young son, whose oval face, black eyes and curving lashes were the ideal beauty of the Persian miniaturist. They had nothing to occupy them, neither book nor pen nor food nor drink. Father and son were lost in the sight and smell of spring." At last Robert Byron had found "that other Persia which so many travellers fell in love with."

The importance of Vita's Persian travels to her development as a gardener was that it enlarged her vision of flower species. She had for long enjoyed the local wild flowers of

Kent, but the richness of the Persian flora was a totally new experience. From now on wild flowers from all over the world, specie bulbs, roses, herbs, climbing plants, with their unique simplicity and innocence, were to be Sackville-West specialities. Tulips from Turkestan, wild roses from Persia, clematis from Western China, were to be valued above the flashiest hybrids, partly for their visual charm, partly for their romantic associations. Her Persian experiences also inspired certain plantings later in her career, for she loved the Persian pots and miniatures, the carpet-making and the craftsmanship, and tried once or twice to interpret this intricacy of pattern in terms of flowers. The thyme lawn at Sissinghurst is an example.

In Persia she tasted the joys of collecting in the wild and small irises, Persian narcissus and Persian tulips and yellow roses were brought home to flower in the garden at Long Barn. "There is a peculiar pleasure" she wrote in *Twelve Days*, "in bringing home plants which one has collected oneself in distant countries. Quite possibly that pleasure may plunge its roots in the fertile soil of vanity . . . there is always the offchance that some true botanist might stray that way, and incline his head obliquely to read the labels. And then I should feel – quite unjustifiably – enrolled in the company of Reginald Farrer and Kingdon-Ward."*

Vita's taste for simple flowers in the garden must have been thwarted from time to time by visits from her mother bringing bedding plants from Knole. Lady Sackville was not blessed with a restrained taste, and once records in her diary "I took lots of plants to Vita, 2 boxes lobelias, irises from Sussex Square, marigolds, geraniums, clarkias, yellow violas". One wonders if Vita, like so many gardeners in similar case, tucked them away inconspicuously under shrubs.

As Vita became more renowned for her gardening, Lady Sackville became intimidated by her famed good taste. The

* In the nineteen-twenties, before the population explosion and protection of the environment became burning topics, there was no ethical objection to collecting plants in the wild.

author has a friend who, as a girl in her twenties, knew Lady Sackville well. One day, in 1928, she was a visitor at Lady Sackville's house in Streatham on a day when Vita was expected for luncheon. Lady Sackville suddenly realized that there was nothing in the garden to impress her daughter. She thrust £40 in notes into her young friend's purse and told her to hurry to Marshall & Snelgrove and buy all the artificial flowers in the shop. The girl returned with boxes full of velvet flowers, wax flowers, even beaded and sequinned flowers, and Lady Sackville stuck them all over the garden. When Vita arrived, dramatic in cloak and sombrero, the garden was brilliant with artificial blooms. Vita's thoughts are not recorded.

There is not much more to relate about Long Barn except that the garden matured and improved. Vita added constantly to her rose collection and in 1926 made rose-covered arches leading from one enclosure to another of which she reported rather nervously to Harold: "although they may sound like a tea-garden, they do not look like it." She often visited nurseries and talked to the nurserymen and worked hard to make the garden lovely for Harold's return from Persia, though she met with some of a gardener's usual disappointments. "It distresses me to think that the irises will not get their usual baking this summer and so will not flower as they should for the return of the prodigal son." In fact, when he did come home in 1927 he was tremendously impressed and found the garden "a different place; wide lawns and tidy edges; tulips and aubrieta, phlox, lilac, irises – a sea of colour."

The Nicolsons' knowledge of gardening grew as vigorously as their plants. There exists a second Long Barn Garden Notebook, kept by Vita, dated 1925–1929, which is far more advanced than the first elementary notebook of 1916. The lists are elaborate, the botanical names are correct, herbs begin to appear in quantity, there are planting plans for every terrace, bank and corner; there are to be a planting of double peaches, walls patterned with ceanothus, arches of honeysuckle. A sketch plan by Harold is slipped into the book giving careful measurements of beds and paths.

Whenever he was in London, Harold made a point of going to the Royal Horticultural Society Flower Shows, where he usually ordered plants, and he once gave a highly entertaining wireless talk about the Spring Show which he had just visited. He concentrated at this show on an exhibit of saxifrages, "a plant which has never quite made up its mind whether it would prefer to be the bath-flannel or the bath-sponge. And yet I am told by those who have come to know a saxifrage really well that it is the gentlest and most insinuating of companions, and that it possesses what gardeners call a 'beautiful habit'."

He dilated in the same talk on the English love of flowers and related how he was once motoring in Germany with a German lady and arguing with her that "nowhere but in England did people make a garden where no garden had existed before. We were at that moment approaching a great building by the roadside which looked like a barracks. To my astonishment I saw that the whole space between the barracks and the road had been dug up and was a mass of wallflower and snapdragon. 'Well, I don't know,' she answered; 'look at these barracks, for instance; you see the German private soldier . . .' By that time we were level with the front gate of the barracks, and could read the inscription painted on a white board by the gate. 'British Rhineland Army', it ran, 'Western Depot. Horne barracks.' And there indeed was a little British Tommy coming out of the gate with a red watering-can in his hand."

The date of that broadcast was March 21st, 1930, but Harold Nicolson had no conception when he spoke that within a few weeks he himself would be embroiled in making, where no garden had existed before, one of the most famous gardens in the world.

For some time the Nicolsons had felt that they might be forced to move from Long Barn because the farmland adjoining was threatened with development and they had begun to look for another house. On April 4th, 1930, Vita, accompanied by her friend Dorothy Wellesley and her younger

RIGHT
Vita at Sissinghurst in 1931.

BELOW
The Rose Garden as it was in 1932.
The yews of the Rondel hedge had just
been planted.

Harold and Vita on the steps of the tower in 1959.

Vita's writing-table in the tower, with a portrait of the Brontë sisters and a photograph of Harold. She liked to have several small vases of flowers on her desk.

son, Nigel, went to see a ruined tower and some broken-down farm buildings in the middle of a derelict field, and being of an intensely romantic nature, she fell in love with them. Standing in the middle of a cabbage patch and looking at the tower tinted golden in the pale afternoon sun, she turned to Nigel and said "I think we shall be happy in this place." She went home and telephoned to Harold to say that she had found the ideal house.

Next day, she took Harold and Ben to see it (Harold recorded: "We go round carefully in the mud. I am cold and calm but I like it!"). For a few weeks they vacillated; Harold's mother was discouraging and Harold not unnaturally got nerves about the cash. "I am terrified of socialist legislation, of not being able to let the fields, of finding that the place is a huge hole into which we pour money", and on one cold, wet day Harold felt that the place looked "big, broken-down and sodden". But he, too, sensed its charm and Vita was persuasive, and by mid-May they had bought it, together with the adjoining farmhouse and five hundred acres of land, for a price of £12,000. The place was called Sissinghurst Castle.

3

Sissinghurst:
The Garden Philosophy

The purchase of Sissinghurst was an act of gambler's madness. It was made at a moment when the Nicolsons' financial fortunes were low. In 1929, Harold decided to resign from the Foreign Office and try his hand at journalism – greater potential rewards but greater risks – and simultaneously Vita renounced the income of £1,600 a year due to her from a trust fund because her mother's increasing belligerence made its acceptance painful. Their capital was small.

But the prospect of so great an adventure was irresistible to both. Here was a creative challenge on a scale they had never attempted before. Vita, still, at thirty-eight, as romantic as in first youth, was spellbound by the castle's beauty and also by its history. In 1554 Cecily, daughter of Sir John Baker, then owner of Sissinghurst, married Sir Thomas Sackville, later 1st Earl of Dorset, and he, in 1586, was presented with the house and lands of Knole by his cousin, Queen Elizabeth. Thus Knole and Sissinghurst had been connected for centuries. Furthermore, Vita was a direct descendant of Sir John Baker in the thirteenth generation, so that Sissinghurst was in her ancestry. Since lineage was an obsession with her, Sissinghurst could be, as no other house, a compensation for the loss of Knole.

For his part Harold, only slightly more cautious, longed to dabble again in his beloved hobby of garden architecture. While they were hesitating, he summed up the pro's and con's in a letter to Vita dated April 24th, 1930:

My view is:

(a) That it is most unwise of us to get Sissinghurst. It costs us £12,000 to buy and will cost another good £15,000 to put it in order. This will mean nearly £30,000 before we have done with it. For £30,000 we could buy a beautiful place replete with park, garage, h. and c., central heating, historical associations, and two lodges l. and r.

(b) That it is most wise of us to buy Sissinghurst. Through its veins pulses the blood of the Sackville dynasty. True it is that it comes through the female line – but then we are both feminist and, after all, Knole came in the same way. It is, for you, an ancestral mansion: that makes up for the company's water and h. and c.

(c) It is in Kent. It is a part of Kent we like. It is self-contained, I could make a lake. The boys could ride.

(d) We like it.

His summing-up was loaded in favour of the adventure, and on May 7th they bought it.

This is a book about the garden at Sissinghurst, not a history of the castle, which has already been written.* It is enough to say here that on the site there had once been a mediaeval house with a moat which was pulled down and rebuilt in Tudor times and then bought by Vita's ancestor, the wealthy statesman, Sir John Baker. This house in turn was almost entirely demolished by his son, Sir Richard Baker, between 1560 and 1570, who left only the low range of Tudor buildings at the entrance. Beyond this he built a vast new Elizabethan mansion round three sides of a square of which each side was some seventy yards long. He also built a tall, slender, free-standing tower and a separate house for the family priest. A later member of the Baker family added a chapel, but from the middle of the 17th century the family

---

* *Sissinghurst Castle*, an illustrated guide, by Nigel Nicolson; copyright of the National Trust.

fortunes declined, and the house fell into decay and met sad vicissitudes.

In the 18th century it was for a time a disgusting prison for the incarceration of French seamen captured in the Seven Years War. (The historian Gibbon was an officer of the guard and hated the place). In 1800 it went back into private hands and was entirely pulled down except for the four buildings which remain today: the Tudor entrance range; the Elizabethan tower; the Elizabethan priest's house; and a tiny portion of the three-sided Elizabethan mansion now known as the South Cottage. These were used from 1796 to 1855 as a workhouse, then degenerated into still worse disrepair and were used as farm buildings. This is what the Nicolsons found in 1930 – the four buildings, all isolated from each other, of which only the entrance range was inhabited and that squalidly shared by cart-horses and farm labourers. The garden was no better than a rubbishy patch of ground thick with weeds and scarred with shabby sheds and broken-down fencing. Nobody could describe it better than Vita herself:

"The site of Sissinghurst was not a new one: it went back to the reign of Henry VIII. This was an advantage in many ways. It meant that some of the Tudor buildings remained as a background: it meant that some high Tudor walls of pink brick remained as the anatomy of the garden-to-be, and two stretches of a much older moat provided a black mirror of quiet water in the distance. The soil had been cultivated for at least four hundred years, and it was not a bad soil to start with, being in the main what is geologically called Tunbridge Wells sand: a somewhat misleading name, since it was not sandy, but consisted of a top-spit of decently friable loam with a clay bottom, if we were so unwise as to turn up the sub-soil two spits deep.

"These were the advantages, and I would not denigrate them. But in self-justification I must also draw attention to the disadvantages. The major nuisance was the truly appalling mess of rubbish to be cleared away before we could undertake any planting at all. The place had been on the market for several years since the death of the last owner, a farmer, who naturally had not regarded the surroundings of the old castle as a garden, but merely as a convenient dump for his rusty iron, or as allotments for his labourers, or as runs for their chickens. The amount of old bedsteads, old plough-shares, old cabbage stalks, old broken-down earth closets, old matted wire, and mountains of sardine tins, all muddled up in a tangle of bindweed, nettles and ground elder, should have sufficed to daunt anybody.

"Yet the place, when I first saw it on a spring day in 1930, caught instantly at my heart and my imagination. I fell in love at first sight. I saw what might be made of it. It was Sleeping Beauty's Garden: but a garden crying out for rescue. It was easy to foresee, even then, what a struggle we should have to redeem it."*

The site of what was to be the garden was about seven acres in size, flat, enclosed on two sides by two remaining arms of the old moat. There were, disappointingly, no plants of value – no old cedar, mulberry or yew. Their total plant inheritance was a grove of nut-trees (Kentish cobs and filberts), some old apple-trees and a quince, though they later found a tangle of a rare old gallica rose now known as 'Sissinghurst Castle'.

Though the site was flat, it was not symmetrical. "The walls were not at all at right angles to one another; the courtyard was not rectangular but coffin-shaped; the Tower was not opposite the main entrance", and there were an infinite number of other oddities which had to be rationalized.

Their assets, then, were four buildings of beautiful mellow brick, part of a moat, various fine walls remaining from the Elizabethan period, and the nut-trees, which they much appreciated as being indigenous to the Kentish scene.

From the beginning Harold and Vita knew the kind of garden they wanted to make, and Harold worked on the production of a comprehensive plan. Being now a gardener of fifteen years experience he knew that the garden-designer

* From an article by V. Sackville-West in The Journal of the Royal Horticultural Society, November, 1953.

"must have his own sketch map clear in his head before he starts to level or to plant." The Nicolsons wanted a garden of formal structure with long vistas leading to focal points. They wanted a garden of an essentially secret and private nature, with enclosures and an element of mystery and surprise. They wanted a garden which would be truly English in character, appropriate for the climate and the surrounding landscape. And they wanted – Vita, particularly – to plant the garden with romantic profusion. Few artistic dreams can ever have been so completely realized.

These, put baldly, were their principles, and it is worth pausing to expand on each in turn.

On *formality*, Harold wrote later* that "the main axis of a garden should be indicated, and indeed emphasized, by rectilinear perspectives, by lines of clipped hedges ending in terminals in the form of statues or stone benches. Opening from the main axis there should be smaller enclosed gardens". Or, in Vita's words* "We agreed entirely on what was to be the main principle of the garden: a combination of long axial walks, running north and south, east and west, usually with terminal points such as a statue or an archway or a pair of sentinel poplars, and the more intimate surprise of small geometrical gardens opening off them, rather as the rooms of an enormous house would open off the arterial corridors."

On *privacy*, Harold wrote, with some wit, "I admit that Versailles, Courances and Villandry are superb achievements of the architectural school of gardening. Yet a garden is intended for the pleasure of its owner and not for ostentation. Nobody could sit with his family on the parterre of Versailles and read the Sunday papers while sipping China tea. Nobody who really cares for flowers can really want them arranged in patterns as if they were carpets from Shiraz or Isfahan. Most civilized people prefer the shade of some dear family

* These quotations are from Harold Nicolson's Introduction to *Great Gardens*, by Peter Coats, published 1963, and from V. Sackville-West's article, *The Garden at Sissinghurst Castle*, in the Royal Horticultural Society Journal, November, 1953. Both were written in retrospect, but the philosophy expressed was already formed in 1930. There were certain mistakes and changes in the making of the garden, but remarkably few. They forged ahead on planned lines.

tree to the opulence of a parterre, displaying its pattern under the wide open sky."*

The idea of enclosures has a further merit besides that of privacy, for it gives the chance to have separate seasonal gardens reaching their peak at different times. Vita wrote: "one of the ideas we had decided on from the first was that the garden with all its separate rooms and sub-sections must be a garden of seasonal features throughout the year; it was large enough to afford the space; we could have a spring garden, March to mid-May; and an early summer garden, May–July; and a late summer garden, July–August; and an autumn garden, September–October. Winter must take care of itself, with a few winter-flowering shrubs and some early bulbs."

On *the Englishness of character*, Harold believed that "our superb climate conditions our style – the English lawn is the basis of our garden design ... The garden designer must recognize that the foundations of any good English garden are water, trees, hedges and lawn". Vita, of course, was delighted that Sissinghurst was "very English, very Kentish, with its distant prospect over woods and cornfields and hop-gardens and the North Downs, and the pointed oast-houses and the great barn", and, always fascinated by words, adopted two local words for two features of the garden. She discovered with "a stab of pleasure" that *rondel* was the Kentish word for the circular hop-drying floor in an oast-house, and adopted the word for the circular lawn they made in the rose garden; and she christened their copse of nut-trees with the local name *nut-plat*. However, it must be pointed out, in contradiction of the "Englishness" of Sissing-hurst, that Vita felt it also had something of the air of a Normandy manor-house.

On *profusion*, Vita is the more eloquent. She wanted "a tumble of roses and honeysuckle, figs and vines. It was a romantic place, and, within the austerity of Harold Nicol-son's straight lines, must be romantically treated". She planned for rich planting and thick underplanting, walls

* *Ibid.*

laced with climbers, many roses, many wild plants, many old-fashioned plants, the whole garden to be furnished with a lavish hand.

What influences formed their philosophy? No work of art springs fully armed from the head of Zeus. There must be antecedents. The influences on Sissinghurst have to be largely inferred, for neither Harold nor Vita wrote an explicit essay on the subject, and one has to ask oneself what they had known, seen and read to affect their conception of a garden.

Knole, certainly, was an influence – not the Knole garden itself, which was mostly lawns and trees, with some conventional flower borders which Vita never liked, but the Englishness of the house and the whole estate. "Knole is above all an English house" wrote Vita in *Knole and the Sackvilles* (1922). "It has the tone of England; it melts into the green of the garden turf, into the tawnier green of the park beyond, with the blue of the pale English sky." And again: "The great Palladian houses of the eighteenth century are *in* England, they are not *of* England." Englishness was one of the qualities they most wanted to achieve at Sissinghurst; hence the Tudor idea of linked enclosures, the English lawns and hedges, the use of native yews and hornbeams, the many smaller indigenous plants, like primroses and violets.

Hidcote? Here is a mystery. Hidcote is the one outstanding English garden earlier than Sissinghurst (it was begun in 1905), composed of separate rooms with high hedges for living walls, and with informal planting within a formal structure. On this, if on any garden, Sissinghurst might have been based. We know that both Harold and Vita thought Hidcote a masterpiece. In 1963 Harold wrote "I should myself rank Hidcote as the best example of this fusion of expectation with the element of surprise", and in 1949 Vita wrote a generous, highly appreciative essay on Hidcote for the Royal Horticultural Society Journal, in which she refers to meeting its creator, Major Lawrence Johnston, "long ago" and to having been his guest "on previous visits". But there is no certain evidence that either Harold or Vita visited Hidcote before 1941. However, the writer thinks it impossible that they should not have seen Hidcote earlier (surely their curiosity would have taken them there?) or at least seen photographs of Sissinghurst's great precursor.

Other gardens which would probably have inspired them are the cloistered enclosures of monasteries and abbeys. They must have seen many on their travels, lovers of architecture that they were, and the antiquity of these gardens would have appealed to their sense of history. In England, monks were growing herbs and flowers when the great lords were still living in fortified castles on windy hilltops.

It *is* known, with certainty, that Vita visited Miss Jekyll's garden, Munstead Wood, for she went with her mother and Sir Edwin Lutyens to see it on August 25th, 1917, commenting politely rather than enthusiastically "not at its best but one can see it must be lovely." In several later writings Vita paid tribute to Miss Jekyll's talent and taste, and some of Miss Jekyll's ideas were adopted at Sissinghurst – notably, nut-trees underplanted with primroses and a decorative orchard. Miss Jekyll was also a doughty advocate of seasonal planting, and both women were artists with colour. But Vita never liked herbaceous borders, Miss Jekyll's speciality, and one cannot think of her as a Jekyll devotee.

William Robinson, on the other hand, author of *The English Flower Garden*, the revolutionary who attacked the falseness and formalism of the Victorian garden, must have had an enormous influence on Vita, who knew him and admired his writing. His words sing out in every corner of Sissinghurst. "Formality is often essential to the plan of a garden but never to the arrangement of its flowers or shrubs" could be Sissinghurst's motto.

Robinson commended such garden ideas as straight lines; blossoming hedges (roses, sweet briar, honeysuckle); creepers and ramblers on a house to clothe the fabric; roses, not trained as standards but well-grouped and underplanted; the loose planting of shrubs in a border; borders crammed with successions of hardy flowers and bulbs; cottage gardens;

climbers rambling up trees, or festooning hedges or creeping through host shrubs; clematis on hollies or even on azaleas. He loved wild roses (like *Rosa brunonii, R. rugosa, R. macrantha*); beauty of form and leaf; an orchard wild garden; flowers near the house in beds and bays; surprises in the garden; woodland plants like Solomon's seal and foxgloves and primroses; rosebeds underplanted with pansies.

He thundered against standard roses; scrollwork; carpet bedding; sham Italian gardens; overcrowded mixed shrubberies; pleached limes.

Almost all Robinson's ideas were adopted and translated at Sissinghurst with one important exception. The Lime Walk in the Spring Garden – an avenue of pleached limes underplanted with spring flowers – might have shocked Robinson. It is the most formal planting in the whole of Sissinghurst and it is significant that the Spring Garden was specifically Harold's garden, not touched by Vita, where he had his own gardener to work with him. Perhaps if Robinson had seen it, he would have been converted. Iconoclasts must always exaggerate, and so frightful was the insensitive geometry of the Victorian garden that, in attacking it and changing the style of the English garden for a century to come, he was forced to overegg the pudding.

There are no other obvious influences on the design of Sissinghurst and even these are partly guesswork. Perhaps works of art they had seen and loved – Persian carpets or Florentine paintings or ruined fragments in Greece – had a hazy influence on some of the planting, and Vita liked to grow plants she had found on her travels, such as the myrtles and pomegranates of Persia, but this should not be pressed too far.

All that is certain is that the Nicolsons knew from the beginning exactly what they wanted to do. Harold and Vita swung into action and started designing and planting even before the agreement to purchase was signed.

4

Into Action

From May, 1930, onward, the chronicler of Sissinghurst is in luck, for there are abundant records of its progress. Harold Nicolson has left a complete list of the dates when each job was done on both the house and the garden – we even know when the trout expert came to inspect the lake and when Vita's terrier had puppies. At the same time (from the beginning of 1930) he began to keep his now celebrated journal,* and in both his journal and his daily letters to Vita when they were apart, there are many revealing references to the garden.

In the first two years, 1930 to 1932, they made a complete plan of the garden which was never basically altered, *a lesson to all gardeners to think before they plant.* They also managed to plant the most important avenues and hedges and some key trees, knowing that every year counts if one wishes to enjoy slow-growing plants in their maturity. And they cleaned and cleared and levelled, a Herculean task which was rewarded almost as soon as it was begun, for in April, 1930, under a tangle of brambles and rubbish, the workmen uncovered the long Elizabethan brick wall which now flanks the Moat Walk.

* *Diaries and Letters*, by Harold Nicolson, are published in book form in three volumes, 1930–1939; 1939–1945; 1945–1962.

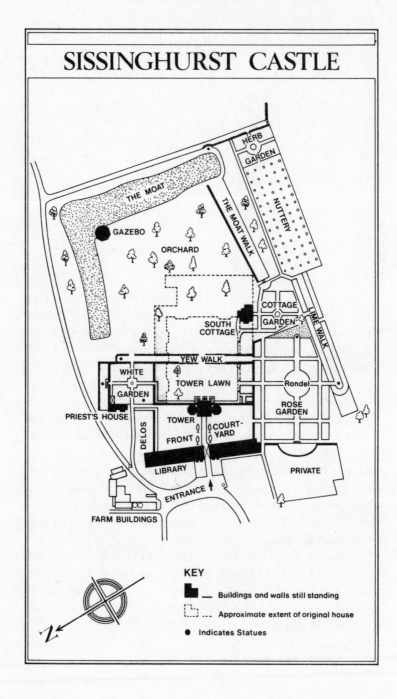

SISSINGHURST CASTLE

THE MOAT

HERB GARDEN

THE MOAT WALK

NUTTERY

GAZEBO

ORCHARD

COTTAGE GARDEN

SOUTH COTTAGE

LIME WALK

YEW WALK

WHITE GARDEN

TOWER LAWN

Rondel

PRIEST'S HOUSE

DELOS

ROSE GARDEN

TOWER

FRONT

COURT-YARD

LIBRARY

PRIVATE

ENTRANCE

FARM BUILDINGS

KEY

■— Buildings and walls still standing

⌐ ⌐ --- Approximate extent of original house

● Indicates Statues

By 1934 the garden had taken recognizable shape and was full of good plants and it was virtually finished by 1939, with the exception of the White Garden, which is post-war. By 1937, only seven years after its birth, the garden was a delight. Harold commented "Lovely summer. The place very beautiful and for the first time the garden looks established."

It was Harold who planned the design using all the paraphernalia of the amateur surveyor – squared paper, balls of string, sticks and tape measures, with a 12-year-old son to act as a living marking-post. Nigel Nicolson remembers standing at the far side of the moat waving a scarf on a bamboo cane while his father tried to find the focal point for a statue. Since the site was quite unsymmetrical, paths had to be twisted, rectangles adjusted, circles bent, enclosures pushed this way and that, to achieve miracles of optical illusion.

The master plan was as follows: There was to be an avenue of trees leading up to the castle entrance, then entry through the archway in the front range of Tudor buildings into a courtyard dominated by the tower. (The archway had been blocked up but was to be re-opened.) One would then pass through the tower into the garden proper in which there were to be two main axial vistas and a number of minor vistas. (Since a description of garden architecture is incomprehensible without a plan, the reader is urged to study the plan opposite, which makes the design clear.)

The first vista runs (approximately) from west to east, from the steps of the tower, across the Tower Lawn, through a gap in the yew hedges, and across the orchard, and ends at a statue of Dionysus placed at the far side of the moat.

The second vista runs across this at right angles. Starting at the north end, it runs from an archway on the boundary between the garden and the open country, through what is now the White Garden, under an arch called Bishops' Gate,* across the Tower Lawn, through the Rondel in the centre of the Rose Garden, and ends at a statue of a Bacchante at the

* The plaque of three Greek bishops which the Nicolsons brought from Constantinople is set in the wall by this gate.

west end of the Lime Walk.

Three important subsidiary vistas are the Lime Walk itself; the Yew Walk, which runs parallel with the second vista; and the Moat Walk, which runs from the Cottage Garden down to the moat and ends at the same statue of Dionysus, who thus does double duty. The Moat Walk is a broad alley on what was centuries ago a third arm of the moat; it is flanked by the moat wall on one side and by a bank of azaleas on the other. The azalea bank cunningly conceals the fact that the nuttery and the moat wall, which "came with the garden" and were unalterable, were not parallel. The bank is not a rectangle but is the shape of a long coffin.

These vistas were, from the beginning, the main bones of the garden. Leading off them Harold planned for many linked enclosures, each of which was to be formal, with straight paths, an interesting centrepiece, such as a pot or urn, and, above all, straight, strong, glorious hedges to act as living walls except where there were existing walls of Elizabethan brick. (Three extra walls were built to complete enclosures where brick seemed more suitable than hedging.) These enclosures are now known as the Front Courtyard, the Tower Lawn, the White Garden (this was originally a rose garden), the Rose and Rondel Garden (originally a kitchen garden), the Lime Walk (also known as the Spring Garden), the Nuttery, the Cottage Garden, the Herb Garden, and the Orchard. There was also an enclosure near the Priest's House called Delos, since it was roughly terraced with fragments of stone collected from all over Sissinghurst, and looked a little like the island of Delos, but it never quite "jelled" and underwent more changes than the other gardens.

Outside the garden proper there are larger, unenclosed plantings, mostly of trees. Harold planned from the beginning for an avenue of poplars leading up to the entrance, and for a lake to be made in the wood at the far end of the garden beyond the moat. It was to be surrounded with water-loving trees and shrubs and to be linked with the moat by another avenue of poplars. The field to the south of the garden was also to be planted with a few good trees.

The complete record of dates kept by Harold Nicolson is too detailed to publish in full and includes the chronology of the house as well as of the garden. Some key dates have been selected to show not only how this particular garden was made but also how a garden *ought* to be made – structure first, trees and hedges next, then the lawns and the smaller plantings. Of course Vita could not resist putting in a few small flowers early on, but they were expendable, and if her plants interfered with the master plan, they had to come out.

The work had to be phased to fit in with the Nicolsons' cash situation, for they were financially stretched until Vita's mother died early in 1936. In the early years there were only two gardeners, a man called George Hayter and his son, but there was also a chauffeur, Jack Copper, to help with the laying of paths, and there never seems to have been a shortage of labour. In the nineteen-thirties, all things were possible. When the Nicolsons wanted to go on main water, the water was brought in a few weeks, and builders and electricians were always hungry for work.

The record for 1930 shows the huge enthusiasm with which the new owners of Sissinghurst went to work. They planted a few flowers before they even signed the contract! In this first year, they decided to make a lake by damming a stream and flooding the two marshy meadows to the south of the castle, and the work was begun. They discovered the moat wall hidden under rubbish and cleared it. They planned for a lawn to the east of the tower, which they called the Tower Lawn. They dug a flower border. They started to dig out dead hedges. They cleared the Nuttery. They planted pinks, rosemary and *Lilium candidum*. They made a pool called the Lion Pond at the south end of the Town Lawn, but it was one of the few structural features which they subsequently scrapped. It is now a sunk garden.

In 1931, they finished the lake, opened the central arch in the entrance, began to make stone paths in the Cottage Garden, made grass paths in the Orchard, turfed the Moat

Walk and the Tower Lawn, cut a vista to the lake, cleared away more of the old rubbishy hedges and cut down elders in the courtyard. They made a half-moon shaped terrace called Sissinghurst Crescent at the east end of the Cottage Garden, with steps leading down to the Moat Walk. In August, they marked out the Rose Garden (now the White Garden), made the paths in September and planted the beds, mostly with shrub roses, in November, the first of all the enclosures to be finished.

In the same year they planted some hardwood trees and many shrubs. They planted a mulberry tree, birches, poplars and weeping willows near the lake and some flowering cherries in the Orchard. Smaller plantings included camellias, magnolias, lilacs, roses, irises, fuchsias, lavender, abutilon, a variety of shrubs, a hedge of sweet briar to divide the Orchard from the South Cottage, water-lilies in the Lion Pond, daffodils in the Orchard, delphiniums and lilies-of-the-valley. A large bed of roses was dug in the garden of the Priest's House.

By the end of the year nearly all the garden had been cleared of rubbish.

1932 was an important year for tree planting. They planted the avenue of poplars which leads up to the entrance, two poplars at the far end of the Moat Walk, another avenue of 36 poplars leading from the moat to the lake. They planted two lime-trees at the castle entrance, a catalpa on the Tower Lawn, the 30 limes of the Lime Walk, the hornbeam hedges behind the limes, and the four Irish yews which stand sentinel in the Front Courtyard. Five acacias were planted round Sissinghurst Crescent.

The yew hedges of the Yew Walk were planted, one row in the spring, the second row in the autumn.

Big plantings of both trees and flowers were made down by the lake: three horse chestnuts, a catalpa, weeping willows, silver birches, dogwood in masses, rhododendrons, sweet briar, Japanese irises, primulas and water-lilies. In the field between the garden and the lake, birches, chestnuts and mountain ash were planted.

ABOVE
The Purple Border with clematis,
campanulas, salvias and many other
plants in a colour range of red, purple
and mauve. The white climbing rose
in the background is *Rosa longicuspis*.

RIGHT
The Nuttery carpeted with primroses and polyanthus.

LEFT
The Bishops' Gate, leading into the
White Garden. The plaque was
brought home by the Nicolsons from
Constantinople in 1914.

BELOW
The White Garden planted entirely
in white, green and silver. The
centre-piece is a frame canopied with
Rosa longicuspis. The pot is Ming.

Progress was made with the planting of shrubs and flowers in the garden itself – the white wisteria which overhangs the moat wall went in, also other wisterias sent by Lady Sackville from her house in Streatham, which she was about to give up, retaining her other house in Brighton; and buddleias, lavender and tree lupins. Foxgloves were planted in the Nuttery (Harold went down to the woods and collected them in a pram), *Iris kaempferi* by the moat, water-lilies in the lake, and irises and primulas on the verges. The most important hedge planting this year was of a circle of yew round the Rondel in the centre of the kitchen garden, which was to be made gradually into the Rose Garden of today.

The work on steps and paths continued, the courtyard paving was finished, and the Nicolsons began to place the ornaments of the garden. The finest of these came by van in March and April from Lady Sackville in Streatham – eight magnificent bronze urns* and two lead vases with covers. The bronze urns were placed on Sissinghurst Crescent and down the Moat Walk and the lead vases went on the tower steps, but they were soon rearranged by the Nicolsons in different positions and were changed again after the war. They now stand as follows: of the bronze urns, four with satyrs heads for handles are outside the castle entrance, two, with sphinx handles, are on the tower steps, and two were sold after the war. The lead vases are on the semi-circular terrace at the west end of today's Rose Garden.

In October, the statue of Dionysus was erected.

In 1933, the Nicolsons were away in the United States for the first four months of the year, but much work had been put in hand and was finished in their absence – a cause of

---

* These urns, the best ornaments at Sissinghurst, came originally from the chateau of Bagatelle, built for Marie Antoinette in 1777 by the Comte d'Artois, later Charles X. In 1835, Bagatelle was bought with its priceless contents by the Marquis of Hertford, who left it to his natural son, Sir Richard Wallace. Sir Richard bequeathed many of the treasures to what is now the Wallace Collection, but he lived for a time at Bagatelle, which he left to his wife, who left it to her secretary, Sir John Murray Scott. Sir John bequeathed some of the contents to his friend and companion of many years, Vita's mother, Lady Sackville.

envy to the modern gardener, who must oversee the laying of every brick or risk disaster. More turf was laid, more paving put down, the woodland thinned and tidied.

Later in the year, they planted more trees by the lake and some poplars along the boundary of the field. They planted the box hedges in the vegetable garden, which is now the Rose Garden. In what was the Rose Garden (today's White Garden) they made the pergola resting on fragments of classical columns which they called the Erectheum, which served as a terrace for outdoor meals.

In 1934, the four Irish yews of the Cottage Garden were planted and some important hedges were made, notably, the yew hedge round the present Herb Garden and box edgings to some of the flower beds.

Harold went again to America and in his absence Vita, with the help of their architect, W. R. Powys, struggled to get suitable materials for a high semi-circular wall which was to enclose a crescent-shaped arbour at the west end of the Rose Garden. Vita sent agonized letters to Harold reporting that they could . . . they couldn't . . . they could after all find bricks worthy to be seen in company with the old Elizabethan bricks of the Tower and the original walls. Bricks were eventually chosen and the wall was built in 1935, but it is not considered one of Sissinghurst's best features. The pointing seems too heavy for the bricks.

Many more flowering trees and shrubs were planted and many lilies, in fact, twice as many lilies as they intended. For Harold ordered 300 *Lilium regale* from a firm in Bath and Vita ordered 300 of the same from another bulb firm. Vita wrote "I am not sorry. It ought to make a show such as has never been seen before. They are all paid for."

A consignment of shrubs from Hillier's was planted, including magnolias, sweet bay and shrub roses.

In 1935 the most important construction work carried out was on the house, the conversion of which was virtually finished in this year. Outside, the riverside drive was made in the wood; in the garden the semi-circular wall mentioned above was finished, more lawns were sown, roses, shrubs, a hornbeam hedge and a holly hedge were planted, and a vine on the Erectheum. Delos, the garden near the Priest's House, was dug.

The statue of a virgin by the Yugoslav sculptor, Rosandic, was placed in the Rose Garden (now the White Garden) under the dining-room window of the Priest's House. This is a lead cast of the walnut original in the library.

In 1936, the last Irish yews were planted, more hedges and roses went in. A big greenhouse and an orchid house were put up. Harold ordered some garden pots from a pottery in Venice. Both Harold and Vita made major plantings. Harold had a concrete path laid between the avenue of limes planted in 1932, thus completing the Lime Walk. He planted long beds on either side of the path with a multitude of spring bulbs and flowers, so that the Lime Walk is alternatively known as the Spring Garden. This garden remained entirely under his control for as long as he lived, and was devoted then, as now, to the flowers of March, April and May, after which it is allowed to rest.

Vita's enormous collection of beautiful and interesting plants grew, she planted many old-fashioned roses and made a gentian bed.

Sissinghurst was already, after a mere six years, becoming celebrated for its beauty and variety.

In 1937, the present Rose Garden surrounding the Rondel was finally cleared of vegetables and planted with shrub and climbing roses. The Rondel hedge had gone in, as has been noted, in 1932.

A Greek altar arrived from Shanganagh Castle, the Irish home of Harold's uncle, Lord Dufferin, and was tried in several places, ending up in Delos, but the Nicolsons did not like it there. It went later into the Orchard. It was one of several which Harold bought in at a sale of the family property.*

* This altar, festooned with garlands held by rams' heads, had been taken to Ireland early in the 19th century by a Nicolson ancestor and erected at Shanganagh in July 1832 to commemorate the Reform Bill. Six years later, the reform enthusiast was disillusioned and put a plaque on the reverse side saying ALAS TO THIS DATE A HUMBUG.

Plans were made for the Orchard. A walk round it was levelled and grassed and the Nicolsons decided to plant the orchard as a wild garden. Musk roses were planted in Delos. A fine Chinese pot of the Ming period which Harold had bought in Egypt was placed in the centre of the small Rose Garden (White Garden), which, as the larger Rondel garden took over as the centre for roses, became a herbaceous garden, with massed delphiniums. The climbing roses, of course, were not moved; there were some on the Priest's house, others growing on a little avenue of almond trees.

Harold reported that the garden looked truly established, exactly fulfilling the traditional theory that a garden can be made in seven years, if good plans are made from the beginning.

In 1938, the Herb Garden was made inside the yew hedges planted in 1934. To begin with, there were only four beds.

In 1938 and 1939, Harold reported that they did "not seem to have done anything beyond letting things grow, which they did enormously."

Then came the war and further developments had to wait for many years. But luckily, when war broke out, the garden had been fully planted, and, though much neglected, the plants grew on.

5

Living at Sissinghurst:
1930 to 1939

The early days at Sissinghurst were not idyllic except, possibly, in Vita's romantic mind. The boys, who later grew to love it, were at first disgusted at losing the friendships and amenities of Long Barn and the regular guests were dismayed at the prospect of no more enjoyable weekends. Raymond Mortimer recalls "we all thought Sissinghurst a gloomy place in hideous flat country, with commonplace cottages and no view, and couldn't think why they wanted it." One of the few people who saw the point of Vita's choice was Virginia Woolf.

The Nicolsons did not move in completely for two years, keeping Long Barn in the meantime, but long before that Vita insisted that they spend camping weekends at the castle. It was dreadfully uncomfortable, but, in the best tradition of the English countrywoman, she was impervious to bad weather and indifferent to bad food. Harold was neither.

The first building to be made habitable was the tower, and they had their first picnic inside it on July 12th, 1930, and spent their first night there on October 18th, sleeping on camp beds and putting up sheets of cardboard in the unglazed windows to keep out the rain. There were no light, no drains, no cooking stove, their table was a packing case and water had to be drawn from a well.

The plan was that, when the conversion was finished, Harold and Vita would have bedrooms and Harold a study in the South Cottage; Vita would have her sitting-room in the tower; and the boys would live in the Priest's House which would also contain the common dining-room and kitchen, a similar arrangement to that at Long Barn – unusual, certainly, but exactly suited to the family character. There would be much tramping back and forth through the garden for meals but no more than at an Oxford college, where strolling across the quad has never been considered a hardship. That there was no guest-room was not an inconvenience. It was deliberate. Vita's writing was always supremely important to her and she wanted, increasingly, the solitude of an ivory tower, only her tower was not ivory, but Elizabethan brick. Gardening, too, was becoming increasingly attractive to both of them and when they were not writing, they wanted to be free for the garden. There can be no doubt that they regarded the absence of spare rooms as an advantage. In 1936 Harold wrote to Vita "Sybil [Colefax] scolded me for not having a spare room at Sissingbags. It seems as if the absence of that bedroom, so she said, was aimed directly at herself. As indeed it was." He meant not only Sybil Colefax herself but people like her, the sophisticated London circle. Vita continued to see a few close friends, but they came for luncheon or tea, and an invitation to sleep in one of the boys' bedrooms during a school term was rare indeed. In general, the London world and Sissinghurst were not to mix.

Vita's love of Sissinghurst had from the beginning the intensity of a religion. She wrote "the heavy golden sunshine enriched the old brick with a kind of patina, and made the tower cast a long shadow across the grass, like the finger of a gigantic sundial veering slowly with the sun. Everything was hushed and drowsy and silent, but for the coo of the white pigeons sitting alone together on the roof." And of the tower in the evening: "the tower sprang like a bewitched and rosy fountain towards the sky . . . they climbed the seventy-six steps of the tower and stood on the leaden flat, leaning their elbows on the parapet, and looking out in silence over the fields, the woods, the hop-gardens, and the lake down in the hollow from which a faint mist was rising."* And in 1931 she wrote, and dedicated to Virginia Woolf, a poem which Harold thought was the best thing she had ever written.

SISSINGHURST

Sissinghurst,
Thursday. To V.W.

A tired swimmer in the waves of time
  I throw my hands up: let the surface close:
Sink down through centuries to another clime,
And buried find the castle and the rose.
    Buried in time and sleep,
      So drowsy, overgrown,
That here the moss is green upon the stone
      And lichen stains the keep.
I've sunk into an image, water-drowned,
Where stirs no wind and penetrates no sound,
Illusive, fragile to a touch, remote,
Foundered within the well of years as deep
As in the waters of a stagnant moat.
Yet in and out of these decaying halls
I move, and not a ripple, not a quiver,
Shakes the reflection though the waters shiver –
My tread is to the same illusion bound.
Here, tall and damask as a summer flower,
Rise the brick gable and the springing tower;
    Invading Nature crawls
With ivied fingers over rosy walls,
    Searching the crevices,
Clasping the mullion, riveting the crack,
Binding the fabric crumbling to attack,

---

* These quotations are from *Family History*, published in 1932. The book is a novel, but the description is an exact one of Sissinghurst.

And questing feelers of the wandering fronds
   Grope for interstices,
Holding this myth together under-seas,
   Anachronistic vagabonds!

And here, by birthright far from present fashion,
As no disturber of the mirrored trance
I move, and to the world above the waters
   Wave my incognisance.

For here, where days and years have lost their number,
I let a plummet down in lieu of date,
And lose myself within a slumber
   Submerged, elate.

For now the apple ripens, now the hop,
And now the clover, now the barley-crop;
Spokes bound upon a wheel forever turning,
Wherewith I turn, no present manner learning;
Cry neither 'Speed your processes!' nor 'Stop!'
I am content to leave the world awry
(Busy with politic perplexity,)
If still the cart-horse at the fall of day
Clumps up the lane to stable and to hay,
And tired men go home from the immense
   Labour and life's expense
That force the harsh recalcitrant waste to yield
Corn and not nettles in the harvest-field;
This husbandry, this castle, and this I
   Moving within the deeps,
Shall be content within our timeless spell,
Assembled fragments of an age gone by,
While still the sower sows, the reaper reaps,
Beneath the snowy mountains of the sky,
And meadows dimple to the village bell.
So plods the stallion up my evening lane
And fills me with a mindless deep repose,
   Wherein I find in chain
The castle, and the pasture, and the rose.

Beauty, and use, and beauty once again
Link up my scattered heart, and shape a scheme
Commensurate with a frustrated dream.
The autumn bonfire smokes across the woods
And reddens in the water of the moat;
As red within the water burns the scythe,
And the moon dwindled to her gibbous tithe
   Follows the sunken sun afloat.
Green is the eastern sky and red the west;
The hop-kilns huddle under pallid hoods;
The waggon stupid stands with upright shaft,
As daily life accepts the night's arrest.
Night like a deeper sea engulfs the land,
The castle, and the meadows, and the farm;
Only the baying watch-dog looks for harm,
And shares his chain towards the lunar brand.

In the high room where tall the shadows tilt
As candle-flames blow crooked in the draught,
The reddened sunset on the panes was spilt,
But now as black as nomad's tent
The night-time and the night of time have blent
Their darkness, and the waters doubly sleep.
Over my head the years and centuries sweep,
   The years of childhood flown,
   The centuries unknown;
I dream; I do not weep.

If Vita's thoughts were consistently romantic, Harold's were usually more bracing, and in an extremely funny broadcast in November, 1930, a few weeks after they had spent their first night camping in the tower, he affectionately debunked his wife's rosy vision of Sissinghurst. The broadcast is so delightful and so relevant that it deserves to be quoted almost in full.

It was a fine night, as English nights go, but it had been raining continuously during the preceding week. The

57

workmen who had so kindly distempered our three rooms
for us had churned the garden path into a morass. Both
Edith [Vita] and myself noticed this morass as we struggled
towards the door weighted down with parcels. "It's
very muddy," she said; "you had better take off your
shoes or else you'll make a mess of the living room." "What,
here?" I asked. "Naturally," she answered, a trifle crisply.

Now it is a tricky business, when carrying a loaf of bread,
two syphons of soda-water, a saucepan, and a bag of eggs,
to take off one's shoes. Especially when one has nowhere
to sit down. So I laid the syphons gently upon the garden
path, and placed the bread beside them. I then squirmed
sideways and took off my right shoe. It was coated with
Kent clay. Edith by then had opened the door of our living
room and I hopped towards it. I stood upon the lintel in
my sock and removed the other shoe. The whole performance was neat, labour-saving and cleanly. "First,"
she said in a brisk pioneer voice, "we must have a light."
I lit a candle. "Now you," said Edith, "make a fire while
I go and air the beds." She went upstairs. I laid down my
muddy, my clayey, shoes beside the door and approached
the fireplace. It was very dark and very cold. I lit several
more candles and groped for firewood. There was no firewood of the small sort, only big wet logs. But I found some
shavings, an old copy of *Punch*, and several little cardboard
boxes which had once contained tins of boot polish. With
these I made a blaze. The logs, confronted by this, I fear,
temporary burst of fire, hissed at me gently.

It was then that I observed that my hands were covered
with clay as a result of taking off my shoes. I noticed also
that I had left large clay finger-marks upon the table, the
front of the fireplace, and on all the candles. I started to
clean the candles carefully before Edith should notice
them. And by then the fire had gone out. "We shall want
some water," she cried from the upper room, "take the
jug."

I shambled into my shoes again – noticing that the fire
had lost its early enthusiasm – and went out into the

muddied night. I knew where the pump was, as I had seen it when we bought the cottage. I did not, however, know, until next morning, that Edith, when she visited the place on Wednesday, had planted a large mass of anemones in a direct line between the doorway and the pump. Nor did I know that the pump was a dilatory pump, having to be worked for five minutes before it spouted. "There's something wrong with the pump," I yelled up at her lighted window. "Nonsense," she answered, and I went on working. As is the way with all sluggards, the pump, once it started, became a cascade. Niagara, in comparison, was a mere soulless trickle. And the jug was so startled at this sudden eruption that it came to pieces in my hand. "Edith," I called to her soothingly, "I have broken the jug." She took it well. "All right," she answered, "take the kettle." I splashed back to the house, being careful to take off my shoes at the lintel. I found the kettle. I put on my shoes again. I returned to the pump, which by now had relapsed into its former indifference. Five minutes' work, and I had filled the kettle. And then I coped again with the fire. There were some dry little sticks in a box in the corner which burnt merrily. Even the logs responded to their advances. I piled them on and piled them on. Edith was annoyed about it when at last she descended. They were, it seems, the garden labels which she had brought down from London to mark the course – the by then I fear somewhat crushed and battered course – hitherto followed by her anemones.

And then we dined. I am not an exacting man, but there are four things which I hate. One is soup from tablets; another is sardines; a third is tongue; and the fourth is cheese in wedges. All these four objects had been selected by Edith for my evening meal. I ate it sparingly. She then said that we must wash up and prepare for breakfast. I went to the pump again and fetched more water. We washed up. Now much as I dislike sardines when they are whole, I dislike them even more when they are remains. It is, I find, a difficult thing to wash up neatly,

˙specially by the light of one candle. "Isn't this delicious?"
said Edith. I agreed that it was and broke my second plate.

"What I like," said Edith on re-entering the living
room, "is the mellow light of candles. So soft it is." It was
so soft, indeed, that I was unable to read and at 9.20 p.m.
I said I would go to bed. I was very wet and very cold.
When I was half undressed, Edith banged at my door and
said I must wash my teeth in soda water. She had had the
well-water analysed and it was full of cyclops; cyclops
were bad for the teeth and gave them typhoid – so I must
wash in soda water. I remembered then that I had left the
syphons in the garden. "I am sorry," I said, "Edith, but
I left the syphons in the train." She was very patient and
I got to bed unwashed. I woke next morning with an acute
sore throat and a sense of duty.

I lit the fire – I pumped the pump – I found the saucepan – I started to boil the eggs. I have no idea what I did
to the eggs, but they behaved in a manner which I have
never witnessed in any egg before. They got beyond themselves; some fissure appeared in the shell: and a huge
ectoplasm of albumen spread out from them like a cumular
cloud. And then the coffee-pot disintegrated when I
touched it; and again we had to wash up.

It was after luncheon that I suggested, humbly, be-
seechingly, that we might perhaps go home. Edith agreed.
She agreed even that next week we should ask a village
maiden to come and help. We motored home in silence.
"Edith," I said to her, "I have an idea." "What idea?"
she asked. "I have an idea that I was not born to be a
settler's husband." "No," she answered, "you were *not*."

Not surprisingly, next time the Nicolsons stayed at Sissinghurst, they put up at the Bull Inn in the village.

As soon as the most acute discomforts were alleviated
(especially after the water was laid on) Sissinghurst became
a source of pure pleasure to Harold as well as to Vita. He

enjoyed his designing enormously, seeing the trees, hedges and paths he had sited fall into position and made many entries in his journal concerning the joys of measuring, fiddling about with the vista problem and placing statues and pots.

Harold continued to live in London during the week, as he had always done, but joined Vita every weekend in Kent. The first thing he would do on arrival at Sissinghurst on a Friday evening, would be to "look round the garden in London suit and with swinging briefcase, the first of all his delights. She, alone all week, would plan and toil, committing to a vast notebook (for ink and paper were her adjutants) her plans, her self-interrogation, and when he came back, she put to him her ideas, her worries, her triumphs and disappointments. 'Come: come and look. What shall we do?'"*

It must not be thought that the Nicolsons' lives were spent in gardening. The most important thing to both of them was literature, coupled in Harold's case with politics, especially after 1935, when he was elected M.P. for West Leicester. Every morning, both of them worked in their rooms, then they met for luncheon, spent the afternoon gardening, and often returned to their writing at night, Harold to type his daily journal, of which a single entry might be two thousand words long. Their letters, too, are mostly about daily events and work, with the children and the garden as minority interests. Creating the garden was a glorious hobby, and it is a tribute to their immense energy that the creation of this sublimely beautiful thing was only a part-time occupation. The Nicolsons may have been feudal, but they were anything but idle. Both were prodigious workers.

To Harold, beset by many career troubles, the garden was not only a hobby, but a perfect solace and escape. One day in March, 1932, when everything was going wrong, he wrote in his diary "Disturbed by these considerations we weed the delphinium bed. A sedentary occupation which gives us the reward of finding one or two delphiniums sprouting among

* *Portrait of a Marriage.*

61

the crow's foot. It is very odd. I do not like weeding in any case. I have a cold coming on. I cannot get a job and am deeply in debt. I foresee no exit from our financial worries. Yet Vita and I are as happy as larks alone together. It is a spring day. Very odd." And in May of the same year "Read the first two chapters of my novel, and am filled with overwhelming disgust. An idle chatter they are – no more. Depressed. Plant water-lilies in the lower lake." At the year's end he recorded that it had been the happiest year of his life. Like all true gardeners he found the garden not only a creative occupation, but a companion and a comfort.

It was also sometimes an occasion for practical jokes, for Harold had a puppyish side to his character. It is surprising that he did not have Sissinghurst equipped with one of those water-squirts which were fashionable with the owners of large gardens in the 17th century.

Lord Gladwyn recalls that he once went to Sissinghurst for lunch on a day when Harold had, to his own annoyance, promised to show some American VIPs round the garden. When the party arrived at a peach-tree in blossom, the Americans were astonished to see a ham lying under the tree and asked why it was there. Harold explained "In America, you have peach-fed hams and in England we have ham-fed peaches." He had put the ham there himself.

When either Harold or Vita was abroad, the traveller was kept in close touch with the progress of the garden by the one at home. Neither made any major decision without the other's consent.

In 1934, Vita wrote to Harold in America about a suggestion for openwork gates in one of the walls and he wrote crisply back "if we had openwork gates we should obtain a magnificent view of the Castle House [the farmhouse], the greenhouse and the Coppers' washing . . . we must have solid oak doors." Later, when she was in France and he at Sissinghurst he wrote "oh God, darling! the beauty of this place in spring! Why did nobody ever tell me about May? By the way, Kennelly is making a path all round the nuttery."

So close was his supervision of the garden that he even

measured the trees and hedges year by year and kept a record of their growth. "Niggs [his son Nigel] and I measured the trees yesterday. The prize goes to the acacia by Sissinghurst Crescent, which has grown two feet." He managed to measure trees up to a height of 27 feet (these were poplars); yew hedges, planted at 2' 6" in 1932, and measured every year, had reached 8' 3" by 1941.

The most agitated letter in their garden correspondence was from Vita to Harold in 1935, when the *Daily Express* printed a rumour that Sissinghurst was haunted. Vita was furious.

Vita liked arranging flowers, especially small bouquets, and always put flowers in Harold's room to greet him, and as soon as there were enough flowers for serious picking, he started to take bunches back with him to London on Mondays. In 1936 he wrote to Vita "it is not to be questioned that irises do not care for the Southern Railway. On the other hand, lupins travel lovely and the syringa does not turn a hair. Yet there must be some way of packing them better . . . I have bought some bigger and better vases to house my flowers. They are such a pleasure to me." Vita, hearing that syringa (he meant philadelphus) travelled well, sent some more the next day.

Sissinghurst was not one continuous success story. There were plenty of teething troubles. There would certainly have been more if Harold had not been such a disciplined planner, but even so, there were accidents and mistakes, as befall lesser gardeners. Plans went wrong. Building constructions proved faulty. Plants died.

From the beginning, there was trouble with the lake. It consisted of an upper and a lower lake divided by a causeway and was probably made in too much of a hurry; anyway, it leaked. It was constantly being patched up and three years after it was first flooded it had to be completely drained and made waterproof.

Then there was the trouble over the high, curved wall at the west end of the Rose Garden, for which the Nicolsons used the architect, W. R. Powys, who was helping them with the conversion of the house. Powys started making the wall with new bricks which Vita said were "harsh, just like any bungalow", and they were treated with cow-tea. This failed to tone them down and a new source of supply was found and the wall was completed. This was not the only time when Powys failed to please. The Nicolsons loved him as a man but thought he had terrible taste. Their own taste in the accessories of a garden, and in the furniture and decoration of a house as well, was for the rustic, the pre-war equivalent of today's taste for "ethnic" fashion and décor, which is much the same thing. They liked hand-craftsmanship and countrified furniture; solid oak doors and heavy wooden door-latches. But sometimes there would be a marble table or an elegant 18th century chair mixed in. The worst adjective in the Nicolsons' vocabulary was "vulgar", ostentation being the cardinal sin. Sometimes poor Mr. Powys overstepped the mark, suggesting wrought-iron latches and nail-studded doors. He was architect to the Society for the Protection of Ancient Buildings, so he was certainly no philistine, but an architect is always in a tricky position when his clients have strong tastes of their own.

Sometime changes had to be made owing to Vita's precipitate planting of trees and shrubs in the middle of Harold's focal points and vistas, but usually she gave way gracefully and they were moved. She nearly ruined what is now the Rose Garden by refusing "to remove the miserable little trees which stand in the way of my design. The romantic temperament as usual obstructing the classic."

More surprisingly, quite a number of the early plantings failed to thrive, perhaps because the soil was heavier or the garden windier than Vita realised. Some of the Irish yews died and had to be replaced. The slips of willow round the lake failed to strike. A rose and a vine succumbed. Some of the poplars planted at the entrance were sickly and were moved to the lake. (The young poplars were always doing a general post. The present avenue leading up to the castle entrance is of trees started in another part of the garden and

ABOVE
A general view of the Rose
Garden. The shrub in the border
is *Kolkwitzia amabilis*, with the
climbing rose Etoile de Hollande
on the wall behind.

RIGHT
A column of *Rosa virginiana plena*
in the Rose Garden; *Allium
albopilosum* in the foreground.

LEFT
Of all Sissinghurst's flowers, the
foremost is the rose. Adelaide
d'Orléans foams over an apple-tree.

BELOW
Allen Chandler curtains the archway
overlooking the Top Courtyard.

moved later. They are called the Fez poplars because the Nicolsons brought them back as cuttings from Morocco in 1934.)

Some of the turf took badly and was taken up and replaced by sown grass. Various lawns and paths were from time to time repaired or relevelled. One error which has caused difficulty ever since is that the yews of the Yew Walk were planted uncomfortably close and have to be cut back very hard but even so, there is barely room for two strollers side by side. All amateur gardeners, however great their experience, tend to plant trees and shrubs too close and Vita confessed later that some of her plantings were over-tight. At one time she had the idea of making the yew alley a yew tunnel and the yews were left unclipped on top, which made them die at the base; but the idea was abandoned.

A few of Harold's plans were discarded as being over-elaborate. There was early talk of a fountain in the Front Courtyard and of a cherry-tree walk leading down to the lake, but both ideas were scrapped. One enclosure, but only one, was a failure, and that was the awkward corner near the Priest's House which they called Delos. There were frequent abortive attempts to replant and re-arrange it and columns and stones were tried there but "looked bad" and were taken away again. One of their earliest ideas, the Lion Pond, was also scrapped, but not until 1939. The other changes, including major changes after the war, were not to correct mistakes, but were the developments of natural evolution.

It must be remembered that until old Lady Sackville died in 1936 the Nicolsons could not always afford the best. For instance, they had to make paths of concrete where they would have preferred York stone. Nor are most of the statues and ornaments of high quality. The bronze urns inherited from Lady Sackville are museum pieces. Some of the pots are fine, especially the Chinese pot in the White Garden. There are some good seats to a Lutyens design. (Lutyens, their friend of Long Barn days, never went to Sissinghurst, but he made a seat for Lady Sackville which was later brought to Sissinghurst and copied.) There are some genuine fragments of classical columns dotted about. The early nineteenth century plaque at the entrance to the White Garden, a carving of three Greek bishops martyred by the Turks, is a charming piece of work. But most of the statues were picked up in junk shops and are without distinction – the Dionysus on the far side of the moat looks particularly depressed. The most interesting piece of sculpture is modern, the lead statue of a virgin in the White Garden. The purpose of the other statues was to mark focal points, and this they did perfectly.

Not only were the Nicolsons sometimes obliged to use inferior materials; there was also a shortage of equipment in the early years. Before Vita ran to a motor mower, the grass was cut by a machine pulled by a pony who wore leather boots to protect the turf from hoof-marks. A donkey called Abdul also helped, who sometimes wore panniers and sometimes pulled a cart, but this was a matter of sentiment rather than economy. Vita, who loved animals, had taken pity on his hard life on a trip to Morocco in 1934 and had had him shipped home.

Even when cash was short, there was always staff. Even before Vita inherited money from Lady Sackville, there were two gardeners at Sissinghurst, a chauffeur, a cook, a lady's-maid and under-servants, and Harold and Vita each had a secretary. In 1937, a third gardener was taken on, a boy of 17 called Sidney Neve, who, as this book goes to press, still works at Sissinghurst, having returned after eight years in the army, and by 1939 there were four gardeners. The Nicolsons were spared the household and garden chores which all but the richest must take on today. This does not detract in any way from their achievement. It means only that, if they conceived an idea, it could be realized. They had the imagination to create a great garden and by their literary work they provided the means. Will such a garden ever be made in England again?

As the years went by and the garden grew up, it became celebrated, and shortly before the war the Nicolsons felt confident enough to open it to the public under the charitable auspices of the National Gardens Scheme. It was open on two days in the summer of 1938, on four days in 1939, on six days in 1940, and thereafter it was open daily throughout the spring and summer. The entrance fee was a shilling, and the proceeds raised £25 14s 6d in the first year. After the war, the proceeds rose to much larger amounts; a generous sum was still given to charity and the rest ploughed back into the garden. The customers, known as "the shillingses", put their coins in a bowl left on a table at the entrance. The gardeners got an extra half-crown for doing Sunday duty.

Vita liked these unknown visitors and much preferred seeing strangers to friends. She would talk gardening for hours to interested outsiders who came to see the plants. Many a visitor, seeing this tall, handsome woman working in the garden, wearing a brown jacket and breeches and with secateurs tucked into her boots, would stop to ask her questions, and she would answer patiently and enjoyed it. Yet she would shun old friends and the social effort their visits involved.

She wrote affectionately about "the shillingses" in an article in the *New Statesman* in 1939. "These mild, gentle men and women who invade one's garden after putting their silver token into the bowl, these true peacemakers, these in-offensive lovers of nature in her gayest form, these homely souls who will travel fifty miles by bus with a fox-terrier on a lead, who will pore over a label, taking notes in a penny note-book – those are some of the people I most gladly welcome and salute. Between them and myself a particular form of courtesy survives, a gardener's courtesy, in a world where courtesy is giving place to rougher things."

It must be reported that Harold, on the other hand, was apt to be brusque with strangers and that many walked away feeling snubbed.

6

The Plants of
Sissinghurst

The Nicolsons finished the major plantings of trees and shrubs in six years and these – the framework of the garden – remain the same today. Though they must have looked pathetically puny in their infancy, the trees and shrubs which mark the garden structure were all well established by the end of 1936. To recapitulate from Chapter Four, they are as follows: The main tree plantings are two avenues of poplars outside the garden, one leading from the farm to the castle entrance, the other, at the far end of the garden, leading from the moat to the lake in the wood. There is also a fringe of poplars beyond the moat. Inside the garden, there is the avenue of pleached limes called the Lime Walk. In the Front Courtyard and the Cottage Garden, there are the sharp punctuation marks of Irish yews; and there are a number of specimen trees, such as the catalpa in the Tower Lawn (a young tree has replaced the original) and the flowering trees in the Orchard. Throughout the garden there are noble hedges of which the Yew Walk and the Yew Rondel are the most spectacular. There are the fine hornbeam hedges flanking the Lime Walk and many other hedges enclosing the "separate rooms" which open off the vistas. These are permanent plantings which can be dated.

It would be a mistake to try to be equally factual about the planting of the shrubs and flowers. This kind of planting is not, and never should be, static. The Nicolsons experimented all the time with shapes and colours, moved whole groups of plants to better places, reinvigorated the garden every season with new varieties and fresh ideas, and if they were still gardening, they would be doing the same today. Their travels, their experiences, their reading, their widening circle of gardening friends, all contributed to the garden's richness. By 1939, some of the best gardeners and nurserymen in England had been to see Sissinghurst, exchanging plants and knowledge with the Nicolsons, so that the plant material became more varied and beautiful every year. Two distinguished gardeners whose help they particularly appreciated were Mrs. Norah Lindsay, who advised them on shrubs, and Captain Collingwood Ingram, the great expert on the genus *Prunus*, whose fine garden at Benenden is only four miles from Sissinghurst. "Cherry" Ingram collected plants extensively all over the world and gave his friend and neighbour Vita many species – one of her favourites was a rosemary which he found in the mountains of Corsica, a variety now known as Benenden Blue. Vita greatly admired his collection of cherries and ordered some of his best varieties for Sissinghurst. Their taste in plants always coincided except in the case of rhododendrons; he could not convert her to his liking for them, or persuade her to grow them at Sissinghurst, with the exception of the azalea group. Harold had trounced her plan to plant them at Long Barn, and his criticism must have stuck.

A full planting history of the garden would be both untraceable and tedious. One can, however, write fully and accurately about the *kind* of plants the Nicolsons were collecting between 1930 and 1939, many of which have been associated with Sissinghurst ever since. There are records of every kind – photographs (many taken by Vita), eye witness accounts by surviving friends, and the Nicolsons' own copious writings. Both wrote about their plants in their letters and diaries and long before the war Vita was beginning to write about plants professionally. Her first flower book, *Some Flowers*, came out in 1937 and she wrote occasional country articles for the *New Statesman*. During the war she wrote a series about Sissinghurst for *Country Life* and soon after the war, in 1947, she began the weekly gardening articles for the *Observer* which became so celebrated and so well-loved.

As the designing of the garden neared completion and the planting became the main task in hand, Vita's role became gradually more important than Harold's. She was a supreme plantsman with a style of her own. There are Sissinghurst plants and Sissinghurst ways of combining plants and Sissinghurst colours and Sissinghurst conceits and fancies. The Sissinghurst style was clear for all to see by 1939 and after the war the planting was resumed, restored, improved, enriched every year until Vita's death in 1962, and after that the tradition was faithfully followed by the gardeners and the family, and subsequently by the National Trust. The garden today, though adapted to new needs, is still Vita's garden.

In the following discussion of Sissinghurst plants, the author cannot always be sure which were planted by 1939 and which are post-war, but it is not material. All were planted in Vita's lifetime, and are the chosen plants which have combined to form the continuous Sissinghurst tradition.

Lavishness

The essence of the Sissinghurst style is profusion. Vita wrote "my liking for gardens to be lavish is an inherent part of my philosophy," and the profusion was achieved in divers ways.

One way was the seasonal idea. "Plant lavishly and with concentration on the given moment, and never mind if you get blanks when the moment has passed." Thus the Spring Garden was planned to be in total flower in March, April and May and would then be left to rest. The spring bulbs and blossom of the Orchard would coincide with it. The Moat Walk, flanked by a bank of scented azaleas, would be at its peak in May, after which the Rose Garden would take over, an explosion of bloom in June and early July. The

Cottage Garden and (after the war) the White Garden would bloom from June until the end of summer. In autumn, the Orchard would have a second season.

Another way to profusion was found by thick planting. "Cram, cram, cram every chink and cranny." Sissinghurst was to be a romantic tumble of plants, with interplanting and underplanting and plants intertwining. The plantings she liked were mixed, though never spotty. She believed in "exaggeration; big groups, big masses; I am sure that it is more effective to plant twelve tulips together than to split them into two groups of six." So her mixtures were bold, with pools of roses, bulbs or shrubs melting into drifts of herbaceous plants – she never cared for the classic, unmixed herbaceous border.

The rosebeds, too, were unorthodox, for among the shrub roses there would be not only mounds of pansies and ferns but clumps of much taller plants – irises, peonies, even *Eremurus robustus*. Small creeping plants like acaenas and dwarf campanulas encroached into the heart of the rosebeds and, except in winter, there was little bare soil to be seen. The whole planting of Sissinghurst was, and still is, voluptuously rich.

The idea of plants, especially climbing things, growing into and through one another (an idea highly approved by William Robinson) added to the profusion, to the sense of the garden being an earthly paradise where plants which were in fact carefully cultivated seemed to be growing by the divine will. Vita grew *Clematis jackmanii* through hedges of sweet briar and let the scarlet nasturtium, *Tropaeolum speciosum*, twine like a serpent among the hornbeams and the yews, occasionally darting out a flame-coloured tongue. Vines and species clematis, roses and honeysuckles, were allowed to ramp through shrubs and hedges and to ramble over walls and trees.

Informality
An essential part of the profusion was an informal way of growing plants. To Vita, Sissinghurst always remained the

Sleeping Beauty's castle, and though she was willing to clear the tangle of a hundred slumbering years she did not want the garden scrubbed clean. It was to be hospitable to wildlings.

Harold and Vita fully agreed on the degree of wildness they liked. They abominated coarse weeds like nettles, docks and ground-elder and dandelions in the lawns, and Harold weeded in the Spring Garden nearly every weekend. On the other hand, Vita liked a lawn "enamelled with daisies" and she loved to find the seedlings of favourite flowers about the garden and would go round marking them with little sticks to save them from being hoed by the gardeners.

Often she left them where they grew. When a stray white Darwin tulip grew up beside an Irish yew, she felt that "nature sometimes betrays a divine instinct for shedding her nurslings in the right place." Columbines were always left to seed themselves, for she liked the surprises resulting from their hybridizing. Seedlings of *Viola labradorica* were saved to found new colonies. Once a *Cotoneaster horizontalis* seeded itself in a perfect position in the right angle of a yew hedge. A seedling of Cheddar pink appeared and was welcome in front of a clump of catmint on top of a wall. A *Gentiana sino-ornata* "wandered from its place just in front of a bush of blue plumbago." A blue poppy seeded under *Rosa moyesii*. A "small pink violet, Coeur d'Alsace, crawled over a group of *Iris reticulata*." And when somebody spilled a packet of blood-red snapdragon seed in the cracks of a path, it was regarded as a happy accident.

Harold was just as tolerant of wild seedlings and wrote a letter from America contrasting the haphazard charm of an English garden with the incurably suburban quality of an American garden, over-tamed and over-trimmed like a municipal park.

Vita's pruning was also characteristic of her taste. A professional gardener might tell you that she underpruned, but she loved to see the hedges sprouting with young growth, the shrub roses billowing or even tangling over the paths, and the wayward natural growth of the Irish yews. She hated to see roses firmly propped or butchered with secateurs, liking to think of the rose "as a wildly blossoming shrub" and believed that even hybrid teas flowered better if they were not cut down, in the approved manner, to the fourth outward-facing bud.

Her climbing and rambler roses, too, were given only the lightest trimming, partly because she hated to tear down the birds'-nests. Harold complained ruefully "I suppose one must take for granted this birds'-nest passion . . . I will have to resign myself to my home being an omelette most of the spring and a guano dump the rest of the time."

Her plants were staked when necessary, but tactfully. She thought peasticks the most unobtrusive way of staking floppy herbaceous plants and her climbers were never nailed too rigidly to their walls.

Roses

Coming down to individual flowers, the rose is certainly Sissinghurst's most brilliant star. If all the other flowers were taken away, Sissinghurst would still be a great garden, and it was perhaps a portent that the only flower the Nicolsons found among the weeds in 1930 was a rose, the clump of *Rosa gallica* in the orchard.

Vita loved shrub roses best and above all, the old roses, and the shrub roses in the Rose Garden round the Rondel make one of the finest collections in the world. Here are musk, damask and cabbage roses, rugosas, bourbons and gallicas, China roses and the Rose de Provins, and many species roses such as *Rosa moyesii, R. farreri* and *R. omeiensis pteracantha*. Many of the old roses are strongly scented, and a wave of fragrance ascends from the Rose Garden in its season, especially on a still summer evening. Vita not only acquired hundreds of old-fashioned roses from specialists like Edward Bunyard of Maidstone and later from Miss Hilda Murrell and Mrs. Constance Spry, but she helped to return some lost roses to cultivation. One was the *Rosa gallica* found in the orchard. Another was Souvenir du Docteur Jamain, that lovely but once rare red hybrid per-

petual, which Vita found neglected in a nursery and was
allowed to take away; she took cuttings and gave some to
rosarians to foster, and now it is widely grown. Miss Murrell
says modestly that she herself saw and received more old
roses at Sissinghurst than she provided.

The romance of the old roses appealed to Vita as much
as their beauty and scent. She liked the roses which look like
flowers from a tapestry, the roses with a long history, like the
dark red Gallic rose probably brought from Persia by the
Arabs in the seventh century, and the roses with evocative
names, like Cardinal de Richelieu, or Comtesse du Cayla,
who was the mistress of Louis XVIII, or Félicité et Perpétue,
called after two unfortunate women who were martyred in
Carthage in A.D. 203.

Rose species she loved for their beautiful small leaves as
well as for their simple flowers. The threepenny-bit Rose,
Rosa farreri persetosa, with tiny pink flowers, was a favourite,
and *R. rubrifolia*, with its purplish ferny foliage, was another.
In 1937 she wrote a charming essay on *Rosa moyesii*, published
in *Some Flowers*, saying that "if ever a plant reflected all that
we had ever felt about the delicacy, lyricism and design of a
Chinese drawing, *Rosa moyesii* is that plant."

The roses were never confined to the Rose Garden (which
started, it will be remembered, in what is now the White
Garden, the roses being transferred to the Rondel Garden in
1937). Roses are planted lavishly throughout Sissinghurst.
There are red and purple-flowered shrub roses in the Purple
Border in the Front Courtyard; white roses in the White
Garden; a circle of little Scotch roses round the classic altar
in the Orchard; thickets of rose species in many odd corners;
a sweet briar hedge in the Orchard; and a hedge of the musk
rose Penelope dividing Delos from the farm lane.

And everywhere there are climbing roses. The South
Cottage is smothered with the creamy clusters of Mme Alfred
Carrière and with the "fantastically floriferous" Mme
Edouard Herriot. All the old walls are laced with climbers
and ramblers intertwined with other shrubs. The Tudor
brick of the entrance range is muffled with scarlet Allen

Chandler and with yellow Gloire de Dijon. The great musk ramblers, *Rosa filipes, R. brunonii* and *R. multiflora* climb up the fruit trees in the orchard and sometimes throttle their hosts in the end, so that the prop falls down and the rose is left to make a flowering mound.

Once she had begun to write about gardening, Vita's influence on other gardens became profound and nurserymen knew that a loving reference to a particular plant in a V. Sackville-West article would create an instant demand. Perhaps she overpraised one of her favourite roses, the towering Chinese climber *R. filipes*, a scented rose with clusters of small white flowers with yellow stamens which Vita made fashionable, for the author has found very similar musk ramblers much easier to grow.

The inventory of climbing roses at Sissinghurst would be impossibly lengthy. Just think of a climbing rose – Etoile de Hollande, François Juranville, Dr. van Fleet, Gloire de Dijon, Paul's Lemon Pillar, or what you will – and you can be sure it is there.

Vita grew almost exclusively shrub roses and climbers, though a few hybrid teas and floribundas with old-fashioned flowers found an honoured place. Vita never cared for the modern type of hybrid tea rose, thinking it stiff and artificial.

Climbing Plants

"I see that we are going to have heaps of wall space for climbing things" wrote Vita in 1930.

One of Sissinghurst's greatest assets was beautiful walls, and in addition to the old walls, Harold built high new walls to complete some of the enclosures. All these were to be the background and shelter for hundreds of climbers. As well as the roses, there were to be vines and figs, honeysuckles and clematis, ceanothus and chaenomeles, magnolias, climbing hydrangeas, wisterias, *Solanum crispum* and *Actinidia kolomikta*.

Many of these are familiar to the average gardener, but Vita, who used an ever-increasing variety of plant material, grew many unusual climbers. She liked the akebias, semi-evergreen twining shrubs with leaves like a shamrock, and grew both *A. quinata* and *A. trifoliata*. She grew *Schizandra rubriflora*, with beautiful nodding crimson flowers, and *Cobaea scandens*, with cup-and-saucer flowers, and *Ipomoea purpurea*, or Morning Glory, and abutilon in many colours. *Abutilon megapotamicum* was a favourite Sackville-West flower, "a ballet dancer, something out of Prince Igor . . . a tight-fitting red bodice with a yellow petticoat springing out below it in flares."

Another rare climber which she planted when the garden was only a few years old was *Mutisia retusa*, a Chilean species, which rewards the planter with a "cloud of pink thrown wildly over the tree at whose feet you have planted it." Vita had learnt from William Robinson that tropical flowers often resent being clamped to a wall and prefer to scramble through shrubs. Robinson "generously understood the secret of growing one plant into another. It was as though he adapted the system of the tropical forests he had never seen to the possibilities of an English garden." This tropical inter-twining was entirely to Vita's taste.

Every year she added to the range of varieties she grew of each genus. When one says "vines were planted in the garden" one means purple-leaved vines and hop-leaved vines and *Vitis coignetiae*, which colours richly in autumn, and grape vines in plenty, and many more.

Irises

After the rose, the iris is perhaps the most important Sissinghurst speciality. Both the Nicolsons had grown to love irises in the Long Barn days, and at Sissinghurst their collection grew.

Many tall bearded irises were planted in spectacular clumps among the shrub roses and in the mixed borders throughout the garden, Vita liking them for their architectural leaves as well as for their flowers. Some smaller irises, too, were grown in the borders, such as the rare *I. chrysographes*, from China, with violet-black falls veined with gold and the copper-red *I. fulva*, a native of North America.

Water-loving irises, like *I. sibirica* and *I. laevigata*, were planted near the moat and by the lake. More numerous still were the plantings of the small and species irises of spring, many of them scented, like *I. reticulata* and the incomparable *I. unguicularis* (*I. stylosa*), pale mauve with feathery markings. There were the tiny, stalkless *I. pumila*, and yellow *I. danfordiae* and the very early *I. histrioides*. *Iris innominata*, a North American native, with flowers ranging from pale buff to deep lilac, flowered extravagantly, and *I. graminea* she grew for picking, for she thought it prettily marked and blessed with a scent like a "sun-warmed greengage." Many of these were grown in the Spring Garden, which was Harold's particular responsibility, is slightly different in character from the other separate gardens, and will have a chapter to itself.

One sad little postscript: the sea-green *Iris persica* which Vita brought home from Persia died, unable to withstand the English climate.

Plant Species

You might expect that a sophisticated person would particularly appreciate sophisticated flowers, but the opposite is nearly always the case. The connoisseur gardener tends to sheer away from gigantic hybrid blooms and to seek his pleasure in plant species, that is, in plants in their original form as found in the wild, or in hybrids which keep close to the plants' true nature.

This was particularly true of the Nicolsons. Their reading and their travels and Vita's country background all combined to nurture their love of wild flowers. The gardening writers Vita most admired, particularly William Robinson and E. A. Bowles, were all enthusiasts for plant species, Bowles being one of the world's experts on the crocus, acclaimed "king and emperor of all the crocuses" by no less a man than Reginald Farrer. Bowles collected hundreds of plants in the wild, particularly in the Alps.

Then, travelling in the world's wild places usually opens the eyes to the beauty of wild flowers. Harold and Vita had seen the extraordinary flora of Persia, the sheets of anemones in Italy, the cyclamen nestling among the ruins in Greece,

the still abundant wild flowers of France, and Vita's childhood had been spent among the field and woodland flowers
of Kent. The natural cycle of the country year had made her
"the scholar of simplicity", a phrase she wrote in *The Land*.

All these experiences contributed to Vita's taste for wild
plants and there is a high proportion of plant species in the
garden. There are plants which belie this – Vita was never a
pedantic gardener and loved to experiment, and when she
needed a spectacular hybrid for a planting scheme, she used
it. But the general mood of the garden is toward the wild
flower and its near relations. "Those vast begonias; those
tree-trunk delphiniums; those mops of chrysanthemums . . .
does anyone really like them, except the growers who get
the gold medals?"

Almost the first flower planting the Nicolsons made was of
coloured primroses and polyanthus in the Nuttery, the idea
occurring to them when they saw how vigorously the primroses grew in their woods. (Even earlier Miss Jekyll had, in
her time, planted a grove of nut-trees with polyanthus.)
They began with one strip of plants and gradually increased
the stock until the whole copse of nuts was covered with a
multi-coloured primrose rug. They also transferred some
wild foxgloves to the Nuttery from the wood.

By the middle nineteen-thirties, they had hundreds of
plant species in the garden. There were species roses and
irises, many tulips and anemones, primulas native to China,
Sikkim and Japan (*P. pulverulenta, P. sikkimensis, P. japonica*),
the cyclamen of Greece, Italy and Persia (she preferred them
to the "improved" cyclamen hybrids of the flowershops),
species crocuses, hellebores, fritillaries, narcissus, campanulas,
orchids, ranunculus, even the simple English woodruff and
the Cheddar pink.

Of course not all plant species are small. The wild plants
of the hotter regions of the world can be enormous, and of
these Vita approved. The Crown Imperial of Asia, *Fritillaria
imperialis*, she loved – she called them "stiff, Gothic-looking
flowers" – with their umbels of orange bells at the top of tall,
straight stalks; and the abutilons of South America and the

tigridias of Mexico and the gorgeous lilies of Japan. The Himalayan lily, *Cardiocrinum giganteum*, found an early place at Sissinghurst and is still an important feature of the White Garden. Vita described it as "too splendid to be called vulgar" and liked to imagine it in its native home "matching her stature against the great fissures and precipices and nameless peaks." (When describing plants, Vita often used the personal pronoun, thinking of plants as people.) Knowing that this lily will grow even in England to ten or twelve feet, she liked to grow it in light woodland.

Cottage Plants

Cottage gardening is a natural extension of gardening with wild plants, and Vita often said that the English have a skill in cottage gardening which amounts to genius. She described Hidcote as "a cottage garden on the most glorified scale", meaning the words as high praise, and Sissinghurst, too, could be described as a series of cottage gardens, always excepting the Lime Walk.

What are cottage plants? Not, certainly, the plants of the farm labourer's garden, for until the end of the last war, he was too poor to grow many flowers, needing his plot for vegetables and chickens. The traditional cottage garden of Christmas cards and calendars would have belonged to the poorer gentry of a village, or perhaps to the schoolmistress or the curate, or to the minor Civil Servant, such as the station-master, the lock-keeper, the post-master or the policeman. Certainly, it is not the traditional cottager who is growing "cottage plants" today. The cottager is growing showy hybrid tea roses, like Peace and Super Star, while the lady of the manor is cultivating the subtler charms of *Rosa rubrifolia*.

By cottage plants, one really means old-fashioned plants, the sort of plants to be found in Gerard's Herbal, and of these Vita planted many. She liked auriculas, which she considered the perfect cottage flower, and rare double primroses, rose plantain and pasque flower, violas and cottage pinks, pansies, alliums, herbs.

She was not particularly interested in the staple of the genuine cottager's garden, vegetables, only caring for epicure vegetables like *mange-tout* peas, sorrel or avocadella. The great French gardener, the Vicomte de Noailles, was a regular visitor to Sissinghurst and recalls that "Vita enjoyed catching me out, especially as I am a Frenchman, by serving some rare vegetable for luncheon that I did not know." She liked small, exquisite portions of vegetables, like the heart of an artichoke or a dish of infant peas.

Scented Flowers

Sissinghurst is a wonderfully fragrant garden and Vita thought that one of the most desirable qualities a plant could have was a good smell. She was intrigued by the elusive nature of scent and said that she wished more was known about it. Why did the same flower sometimes give out scent in the morning and sometimes in the evening, sometimes on a cold day, and sometimes in the hot sun? She realized that some flowers puff out scent all the time while others, especially herbs, need to be crushed or brought into a warm room to release their odours.

Of the plants which positively throw their scent at you, Vita grew hundreds, perhaps thousands, of varieties. The bank of azaleas which flanks the Moat Walk simmers with scent in May. The Rose Garden is rich with scent in June and early July; of all her scented roses, she thought the best was the rugosa rose, Blanc Double de Coubert. She liked scented plants as different as balsam poplar and sweet briar, the showy *Lilium auratum* and the humble Cheddar pink. She liked the scent of box hedging in the sun, of night-scented stocks after sunset, a bed of warm wallflowers, a little tree of vanilla-scented *Azara microphylla* in spring, a whiff of witch-hazel in winter. Characteristically, she thought that the best scent of all was that of wild bluebells in a wood.

She planted many honeysuckles on the walls at Sissinghurst, many lilies in the borders, many scented shrubs like *Osmanthus delavayi*, myrtle, and the scented viburnums. And she particularly liked flowers which she could pick on cold

ABOVE
Where Sissinghurst begins.
The entrance range is Tudor,
of fine mellow brick. A path
through the central archway
leads into a courtyard
dominated by the lofty
Elizabethan tower.

RIGHT
Where Sissinghurst ends. The
garden is bounded by a moat
fringed with ancient oaks and
with poplars and hedges
planted by the Nicolsons.

The Priest's House overlooks the White Garden to the east and, to the west, has a serene view of the Weald of Kent.

days in early spring and bring indoors to scent the rooms, like *Daphne odora*, winter-sweet, the small scented irises and jonquils and the tiny Pyrenean narcissus, *N. juncifolius*.

Of herbal plants, there were many all over the garden, and in 1938 Vita made a special Herb Garden inside the living walls of yew hedging which had been planted four years earlier. She started with four simple beds and a "mixed dozen" of herbs, only three in each bed, though they soon clumped up and further herbs were added. It was not until after the war that the design was elaborated and the space cut into twenty small beds divided by narrow paths, all planted with more than a hundred different herbs – many varieties of thymes and melilots, sages and rosemary, fennel and garlic, spicy curry plant, tangy Cologne mint, caraway and woad. Nigel Nicolson recalls that sometimes Vita would sit in the Herb Garden, shut her eyes, and ask him to bring her a herb to identify, and that she nearly always got it right. It is curious that E. A. Bowles had the same acute sense of smell.

Some of the scented flowers went into *pot pourri*, which was made at Sissinghurst from an old recipe which had been followed at Knole since the eighteenth century, when it was concocted by Lady Betty Germaine, a prim little widow who had rooms at Knole in the time of George I and George II. The recipe involves the drying of double violets, rose leaves, lavender, myrtle flowers, verbena, bay leaves, rosemary, balm, musk and geranium, which were then stored in jars with bay salt and many spices.*

Winter Flowers

Vita Sackville-West wrote two long poems about the country, *The Land* (published 1926) and *The Garden* (1946). Each was divided into four sections called after the four seasons, and in each the cycle of the year began with winter. Vita did not entirely dread the winter, but thought of it as a cradle for spring. She found many pleasures in the garden in winter –

---

* See *Knole and the Sackvilles*, by V. Sackville-West (1922).

the sight of pushing young leaves and buds, the frost breaking up the rough-dug earth, the dangle of catkins from bare boughs, not to mention the winter joys of day-dreaming about gardens in Southern Europe and studying catalogues by the fire. At Sissinghurst, she grew all the winter-flowering plants which are hardy in England.

Their catalogue is now well-known but it was not when she started planting them. Winter jasmine and laurustinus were almost the only widely grown winter flowers, and it was largely due to her influence that thousands of English gardeners now grow hellebores and witch-hazel, *Iris unguicularis* and *Prunus subhirtella autumnalis*.

She grew all the winter-flowering shrubs: the winter prunus, the mahonias, *Chimonanthus fragrans*, *Hamamelis mollis*, the early daphnes, *Viburnum fragrans*, winter jasmine, the winter honeysuckles, *Cornus mas* and even the common flowering currant, because it could be picked in February and forced into flower.

She grew the winter hellebores, like *H. niger*, the Christmas rose, and the handsome, green-flowered *H. corsicus*, which she likened to "a miniature pale green water-lily", and thousands of early bulbs – snowdrops, aconites, irises and the early crocuses, like *C. tomasinianus*, which flower before the big Dutch hybrids. Friends recall that in every month of the year "there was always something out".

Vita particularly liked to pick a bunch of flowers for the house from all the freak, scattered blooms she could find on a winter's day and wrote about it in *The Garden*.

> But these your winter bunches, jealously
> Picked on a February morning, they
> Are dearer than the plenteous summer. See,
> One coloured primrose growing from a clump,
> One Lenten rose, one golden aconite,
> Dog Toby in his ruff, with varnish bright,
> One sprig of daphne, roseate or white,
> One violet beneath a mossy stump,
> One gold and purple iris, brave but small

Child of the Caucasus, and bind them all
Into a tussie-mussie packed and tight
And envy not the orchid's rich delight.

Plants at Eye Level

Vita Sackville-West loved *looking into* plants. She would observe with rare sensitivity the form and colours and texture of a flower, and liked to plant flowers of particular delicacy where this beauty could best be seen. Her friend, Mrs. Alvilde Lees-Milne, herself a superb gardener, first drew attention to this quality of Vita's planting and wrote of her "Few people, unless they are painting a flower in detail, or are botanists dissecting it, know plants in this way." *

Sometimes the best way to look into a flower is to plant it near to eye level, and many plants at Sissinghurst, especially small ones and flowers of bell or trumpet shape, are planted off the ground in pots, troughs, sinks, urns and coppers. Vita liked flowers in pots not only because she could then look into them but also because pot gardening is such a feature of the Mediterranean countries which she knew so well.

Liking to observe flowers at close quarters, she became increasingly interested in her greenhouses. There she could peer closely at her flowers growing in pots and pans on the staging, could study the exquisite green marks on a snowdrop or the little squares on a fritillary. For the same reason she preferred small nosegays in the house to big "arrangements" and often had three or four small vases of flowers on her desk and perhaps a pot or two of bulbs.

She found other ways of growing plants so that they could be seen at close quarters. She grew fond of alpines and planted many among the rocks of the Delos garden. She trained clematis horizontally over an openwork table so that she could "gaze right down into the upturned face of the flower instead of having to crane your neck to observe the tangle of colour hanging perhaps ten or twenty feet above your head.

* In an article on Sissinghurst in The Journal of the Royal Horticultural Society, September, 1966.

The full beauty of the flower is then exposed to you." And she liked the smaller climbing shrubs as well as the high scramblers, so that she could pause and look closely at their flowers as she passed by. She was never the sort of landscape gardener who is interested only in mass effects. Each flower was to be intimately known.

Colours and Colour Schemes

"Vita only likes flowers which are brown and difficult to grow" Harold would say, commenting on the subtlety of his wife's colour taste, his own being somewhat less recherché. Vita's preference was always for flowers of delicate and un-usual colour, the greens, the silvers, the shades of cream and white, the dusky reds rather than the strident scarlets, the softer pinks and yellows. Perhaps *Humea elegans*, the Incense Plant, sums up her subtle colour sense as well as any plant, reddish brown and strange green, feathery, smokily scented, standing tall in large pots beside doorways or on steps.

She created a whole fashion for green flowers, rediscovering many which were little grown before the last war though most connoisseurs collect them avidly today. She grew the green rose, *Rosa chinensis viridiflora* and the green *Ixia viridiflora*, and many hellebores and euphorbias and Solomon's Seal and the greenish-pink *Astrantia major*.

From the earliest days of the garden, she grew white flowers in legions, from giant lilies to the miniscule sweet woodruff, from white roses climbing to the rooftop to white jasmine for the house.

Other characteristic colours of the garden were the mauve of *Anemone japonica* and the veiled pink of *Primula pulverulenta* of which Vita wrote "to compare it with the pink of peach-blossom would be to suggest something far too crude, with the pink of apple-blossom something far too washy, with the pink of a sunset cloud something far too pink; nor is there any rose which will give me the precise shade I want. It really suggests a far deeper pink which has been dusted over with chalk." She loved the meadow fritillary for the same reason, for putting "a damask shadow over the grass, as though dusk were falling under a thunder-cloud that veiled the setting sun."

Harold's colour sense suffered from no such inhibitions. He liked warm colours. His spring border glowed with scarlet anemones and bright blue muscari and red and orange tulips.

He also chose the colour scheme for the Cottage Garden, which his own study overlooked, and this was and is planted throughout the summer with sunset coloured flowers. "The Cottage Garden is ablaze with yellow and orange and red" he wrote with delight. And he loved the brilliant colours of "an enchanted garden" he saw in Mexico, rich with tropical creepers in magenta, scarlet and blue, with splashes of Morning Glory, jacaranda and hibiscus.

Both of them liked to group together flowers in the same colour range. The Cottage Garden kept to the sunset range throughout its long season, roughly from June to October. The big flower border at the north end of the Front Courtyard was planted as a purple border with shrubs, roses, clematis, herbaceous plants, biennials, bulbs, all in shades of purple, red and mauve. In the Rose Garden, Vita massed the deep purple roses together – Cardinal de Richelieu, Roseraie de l'Hay, Tuscany, Gypsy Boy – instead of spotting them about to make contrasts as a less sensitive gardener might do.

Quite early in their lives, they conceived the idea of going beyond a one-colour border, and making a one-colour garden. They had tried it in a small way at Long Barn. At Sissinghurst the Cottage Garden is an example on a larger scale. The conception was most triumphantly realized in the White Garden, which was made after the war and will be discussed in its place. But the idea of an all-white garden came to Vita as early as 1939, when the war had barely started.

This is not to say that Vita *only* liked muted colours. When she chose a brilliant flower she planted it boldly and in mass. Her bed of *Gentiana sino-ornata* was a rectangular pool of blue. Her thyme lawn was a magenta carpet. She liked bright red roses like Ulrich Brunner and *Rosa moyesii* provided they had old-fashioned or single flowers. She had a surprising weakness for Red Hot Poker. But she did not like herbaceous borders gay with crude mixtures of lupins, poppies and Golden Rod. Her taste was always for mystery – for colour half-veiled.

Tender Plants

Though Vita positively hated "bedding schemes", with biennials planted in regimental rows, she grew many half-hardy plants, transferring them from the greenhouses in early summer. Sissinghurst was not a permanently planted garden of hardy plants like, for instance, Mrs. Margery Fish's garden made after the war at East Lambrook Manor. (Mrs. Fish never had a greenhouse.)

At Sissinghurst, many tender shrubs were grown in large pots and moved into shelter for the winter and abutilons, scented-leaved geraniums, *Venidio-arctotis*, fuchsias, *Mimulus glutinosus*, *Teucrium fruticans*, *Aster pappei*, *Cobaea scandens* and heliotrope were some of many half-hardy plants which gave the garden botanical interest and exotic beauty.

Only the Best

Although Vita liked profusion, lavishness and interplanting, and used a very wide range of plant material, it must be stressed that she was highly discriminating. In her own garden, bad plants were ruthlessly eliminated and poor forms discarded in favour of better forms, and her advice to other gardeners was always *"grow only the best"*.

On June 8th, 1937, Harold wrote to her "I think the secret of your gardening is simply that you have the courage to abolish ugly or unsuccessful flowers." Perhaps of all the lessons to be learned at Sissinghurst, this is the greatest.

7

The Lime Walk

The Lime Walk (known alternatively as the Spring Garden) is the only one of Sissinghurst's separate gardens which is not in any sense cottagey. It is mathematically planned like a French garden and depends for its effect on exact spacing and perfect trimming. It was exclusively Harold's garden and in later years he had his own gardener to work with him there. He himself did much of the planting and weeding (he planted nearly all the bulbs himself and wrote the labels), and his diaries are punctuated with the entry "weeded Spring Garden". This patient task seemed to purge him of the anxieties of his London week.

The Lime Walk consists of an avenue of thirty lime-trees, fifteen each side, which were planted early in the history of the garden, in November, 1932. Soon afterwards two parallel hornbeam hedges were planted outside the limes. For several years the ground under the trees remained as rough field but in 1936 the alley between the trees was paved and borders were dug between the trees and the hedges.

These flower borders were planted entirely with spring bulbs and flowers planned to bloom in March, April and May. Since there was to be no succession of summer flowers the spring beds could be a solid carpet exquisitely patterned with primroses and narcissus, scillas and anemones, violets and small tulips, and all the fresh, delicate flowers of the budding year.

The design of the garden is intricate. The paving is wider than the avenue of trees and each tree stands in a square of soil cut out of the paving. Each square has its own planting of spring flowers. Large pots from Tuscany, planted with bulbs and clematis, are placed at regular intervals along the Walk and a female statue is sited in the bay at the west end.

No other garden at Sissinghurst is as formal as this and no other garden is quite so seasonally planned. When spring is over, there is nothing to be seen except the beautiful limes themselves which form a green colonnade. Harold seems to have loved spring flowers above all others. In April 1936 he wrote to Vita with enthusiasm "we must get jonquils for our new Unter den Linden border. I am looking forward to that border enormously. I really think that if we take trouble about it, we shall make our spring garden the loveliest in England."

He set about his task with military precision. The florescence of the Lime Walk, which looks so spontaneous, as though a Botticelli goddess had passed that way flinging flowers as she went, is the reward of meticulous planning. Harold kept special notebooks on the Spring Garden, of which three, kept during the war years, survive. In these he mapped out the garden on squared paper, all to scale, numbered the trees from 1 to 30, and gave each section of border between the trees a page to itself. He annotated these little maps with practical jottings, planting lists and a running commentary on the state of play. For instance the page between Tree 8 and Tree 9 would read: "At back, forsythia, tall tulips. In front very good mixture of primroses and anemones, but they are not thick enough. Just fill up. Under Tree 8: *Narcissus nanus*, leave. Pot: v. bad muscari, empty and fill up. Tree 9: good anemones here. Put cotton on primroses. Fritillaries sparse. Get some cuttings of the yellow wallflowers near the cottage."

In the last of the notebooks he graduated to an elaborate

' dating system by which every plant was entered on a calendar and given weekly marks from 1 to 10, 1 indicating its budding date, 5 its summit of flowering, 10 its collapse. One notes that in 1955 the erythroniums held their peak for five weeks, from April 2nd to May 8th, the Crown Imperials had only one peak week, and the scillas and cyclamen never got top marks at all. The omphalodes were marked 5 on April 24th, May 1st and May 8th.

The interest of the notebooks is that they reveal a degree of method rarely reached by the amateur; the lives of hundreds of flowers were recorded with scientific exactitude.

The notebooks also show how fluid the planting was, changing every year. Nothing was left to jog along on its own. The tapestry was rewoven every spring in the search for perfection.

The variety of plants Harold grew in the Lime Walk is astonishing. There are more than a hundred varieties listed in one notebook alone – many auriculas, many narcissus, many fritillaries, tulips, saxifrages, irises, cyclamen, primroses, gentians. Taking anemones only, he grew *A. ranunculoides, A. blanda atrocoerulea, A. nemorosa allenii, A.* Creagh Castle, *A. fulgens, A. pavonina, A. nemorosa robinsoniana, A. pulsatilla* (white and pink), *A.* Caen and *A. sylvestris.*

As well as planting and weeding, Harold sometimes had a go at pleaching the limes. He had been told by a Belgian gardener "il faut être impitoyable" and knew that though the trees would look harshly amputated after their autumn pleaching, they would burst forth in abundant leaf in spring. The English as a nation have a distaste for pleaching and do not understand that the shady canopy of leaves they sit under in some provençal square on a sizzling summer day is the product of hard pruning and strict training, but Harold was not so insular.

When he reached middle age, he would still work on the limes himself, which made Vita nervous. In 1944 he wrote to his sons "Mummy hates ladders. She has an idea that I ought to fix the bottom of the ladder in a crack of the pavement so that it will not slip outwards. She has an idea that if the ladder rests slantwise so that my full weight as I climb up is thrown upon the lime-trees, either the ladder or the lime-tree will break. She has an idea that greater safety would be secured if the ladder stood somehow on its end so that the weight of my body would fall upon the rungs and not upon the trees. I pointed out to her gently that in such a posture the ladder might leave the limes and fall backwards. 'You don't understand', she said: 'I can't explain, but it is as simple as hydraulics.' The latter branch of science is not one of the departments of knowledge on which your mother is really authoritative or even sane. But I did not say so. I merely said that a ladder which stands on its toes is apt to fall backwards, a very dangerous thing to do. She said that I was a physical imbecile. And I confess that when I had finished the lime-walk, it looked as if a giraffe had strayed into the garden and taken large munches out of the trees.''

Vita remained unconvinced that Harold and a ladder were safe companions, justifiably, since he twice fell through the branches of the limes, once breaking his spectacles. She implored her friend the Vicomte de Noailles to undertake the task of explaining to Harold that he was no longer young.

But this is anticipating the story of Sissinghurst during the war. The survival of the wartime notebooks on the Spring Garden led the writer on, for the earlier notebooks have disappeared. Without a doubt they were equally meticulous and without a doubt the Lime Walk had reached near-perfection by 1939, for the limes were planted early and the little bulbs and plants of spring are soon established.

8

The War Years:
1939 to 1945

Physically, Sissinghurst was exposed to the heat of World War II. It was in a vulnerable corner of England. The dog-fights of the Battle of Britain were fought overhead. Had the German invasion been launched, the Kent coast provided the likeliest landing-places. When the V1s and V2s started, Kent was first on their hateful path. "Night after night the bombers streamed overhead to attack London, or, in the opposite direction, the cities of Germany and France. The farm, castle and garden were spattered with the débris of the air-battles. Bombs and parachutists fell in the neighbour-ing fields. On one occasion a German bomber, crashing in flames, missed the Elizabethan tower by only a few yards."*

The Nicolson family, too, was deeply involved in the war. Both Ben and Nigel joined the army in 1939 and were posted overseas within three weeks of each other in 1942, Ben to Cairo with the Intelligence Corps, Nigel to Tunisia with the Grenadier Guards. Later, both fought in Italy.

Harold continued to work in London through the war, as an M.P., as a junior member of the Government for one year and then as a Governor of the B.B.C., and as a liaison man

* Introduction by Nigel Nicolson to Harold Nicolson's *Diaries and Letters*, Vol. II.

with the Free French; his work took him abroad to France, Sweden and North Africa. Vita joined the Kent Committee of the Women's Land Army.

Naturally, the garden suffered. The staff was much reduced, all the gardeners being called up except one who was exempt. The head gardener, John Vass, who had gone to Sissinghurst shortly before the war, went into the R.A.F. in 1941, his parting request being "look after the hedges. We can get the rest back later." The remaining gardener was joined by a Land Girl and these two, with Vita, kept up the garden as best they could, though much had to be let go. The trim lawns went unmown and the tapestries of flowers were stained with weeds. The moat became choked with reeds and the lake with bulrushes. A bank of the moat caved in. The Nuttery became an untended tangle.

Yet, for all the explosions round about, Sissinghurst retained much of its atmosphere of the Sleeping Beauty's Castle. It was still a private world. Harold continued to join Vita for most weekends, enjoying his own special flowers in the Spring Garden and the Cottage Garden, breakfasting in the garden on fine days, bathing in the lake in summer, and taking bunches of flowers back to London to enjoy during the week. "I love when you go off with the plumber's basket spilling its récolte" she wrote in 1943 . . . "I love you having bits of Sissinghurst to take with you, and I feel rather proud of my floraison unaided by any Vass." On various occasions, Harold took back violets, roses, prunus, irises, honeysuckle and dark plum, which he used to dose with aspirin in the vases. Once he reported "the stylosa have unfurled themselves quite beautifully. It is as if all the Ladies at Longchamps had suddenly unfurled pale blue sunshades."

Vita continued to write prolifically in her ivory tower, publishing two major works during the war, one biographical, *The Eagle and the Dove*, a comparison of the lives of two saints, St. Teresa of Avila and St. Thérèse of Lisieux, the other her long poem, *The Garden*, a successor in style and scope to *The Land*. She found it much more difficult than *The Land*, "because the inherent dignity of agriculture is lacking, and seed-boxes are not so romantic as tilth," and worked on it for nearly four years. In spite of the weeds, the garden still produced beautiful flowers and luxurious vegetables and fruit – there were asparagus, new peas, plums, grapes, nectarines, peaches. Nobody commandeered the orchard to make a cabbage field and no tractor ploughed up the Lime Walk. Fortunately for posterity, all the permanent features of the garden and the main trees and hedges went unscathed.

All through the war, Vita worked harder than ever in the garden, as did Harold when he could. She herself scythed in the orchard, slashed thistles by the lake by moonlight, helped Harold to clip hedges and trees. She worked in the greenhouses and maintained the roses and other permanent plants.

During the first nine months of war – the Phoney War – she continued to plan garden improvements as she had always done. In December, 1939, the Lion Pond was drained and she thought of planting a White Garden there: "all white flowers, with some clumps of very pale pink. White clematis, white lavender, white agapanthus, white double primroses, white anemones, white camellias, white lilies including *giganteum* in one corner, and the pink Bartley Strain *Primula pulverulenta*." (This was accomplished ten years later). At Christmas she gave house room to the alpine collection of a neighbour who was called up and promised to care for his treasures. She called them her "wartime evacuees." That winter was bitter and she mourned some plants killed by the frosts and resolved to take more cuttings in future years.

Her eye for the romantic remained undimmed. In May, 1940, she wrote to Harold "the only nice thing that comes out of the war is that we now have a guard on top of the tower. In a steel helmet and rifle he looks most picturesque over the parapet." During that fine, dry summer, she cultivated the flowers to a high standard and wrote of "a softness about the air, a scent of musk and hay, a scent borne from the great white lilies and the tumbling roses." In August, Harold recorded that "the cottage garden is ablaze with yellow and orange and red. A real triumph of gardening." The summer at Sissinghurst had been passed to the background music of gunfire and the wail of sirens across the fields, but the garden retained its spell.

Two years later, Harold was still producing garden plans of a sensible and modest kind. In September, 1942, he wrote "I am thinking about the garden. We can't make it *look* very nice except for May, June and July. There is no hope of us being able to make an August or autumn garden . . . I think we should concentrate on increasing what does well. More elaboration of our own stock. Now, all annuals and biennials involve more work than we, with our present resources, can perform. Cut them out. Away with antirrhinums. But we can legislate for 1946, grow seeds and take cuttings. More forsythia, more magnolia, more kerria, more fuchsia – all the things that entail comparatively slight trouble and mean beauty in 1946." In this same year, the Nicolsons planted quite a few trees, including a tulip-tree, a magnolia, a *Quercus coccinea* and an avenue of ten sweet cherries in the orchard.

Even at this dark period of the war the Nicolsons lost none of their intellectual and aristocratic aloofness. Vita frankly hated her work for the Women's Land Army as a tiresome distraction from her literary work on *The Eagle and The Dove*. "This afternoon I must go touring after land-girls, blast them" she wrote in 1943. And again "bad land girls giving a good deal of trouble". And again "I was deep in St. John of the Cross when people began to arrive. First came a land-girl, wanting me to charge her wireless battery." And again "I am wishing that neither the W.L.A. nor its hostels had ever been invented, after being sent for no less than four times during the morning, and being asked to produce various domestic utensils which I do not even know by name . . . What I dislike most about bedint* women is the absolute gusto with which they fling themselves into practical diffi-culties; to them, a missing pie-dish is as much of an excite-ment as if the entire contents of the British Museum dis-appeared during the night."

---

* A family word meaning uncultivated or "common".

At one point Harold grew quite worried about her absorption in her saints. "I hope the Spring is not going to be too early this year. In the first place, I hate unseasonable weather and in the second place all the little things may get a pinch on their noses. I also hope that my Saint does not suddenly become one. Think of the bore of her attributing to the stigmata what were merely the scratches of a rose bush. Think of the bore if the devout made pilgrimages to Sissingbags and bought rosaries and little bundles of hyssop in the porch! But I do delight in the fact that you are interested in the book."

The Nicolsons did not like the army any better than the land girls. No surge of democratic feeling made them think of the private soldier as their brother. There was an extraordinary episode at Sissinghurst at the end of 1942, at the height of the North African campaign, which Harold recorded in a letter to Ben and Nigel without a tremor of guilt. Since it concerns onions, it should take its place in the history of the garden.

"The military arrived at Sissinghurst. It consisted of the Headquarters of a tank Brigade on exercise, heralded by a young officer of the name of Rubinstein. Recalling how but three days before I had stood in tribute to the martyred Jews of Poland, I was most polite to Captain Rubinstein. His parents, it appeared, live in Leicester. He told us that his Brigadier, plus five officers plus cook plus batmen, would appear by tea-time and wanted to stay the night. We showed him the brew-house, the oast-houses, Nigel's room, Ben's room and the loft beyond. He said that it would do nicely, and departed to inform his Headquarters what a pleasant little welcome was being prepared.

"It was at that moment that Mummy remembered the onions stored on the floor of the loft. They number between two and three thousand. She said that the Army always stole onions and that we must remove them at any cost before they arrived. I said that we were only having a Brigadier and his officers, and that (a) they would probably not want to steal more than three onions each, and (b) we should not miss them much if they did. She said that you could never tell with officers nowadays, so many of them were promoted from the ranks. So we got three sacks and two shovels and all after- noon till darkness came we carried the sacks across to the Priest's House and spread them on the floor of Pat's room. We had scarcely finished with the last onion when the Brigadier appeared. He was a nice well-behaved man and looked so little like an onion-stealer that Mummy at once asked him to dinner.''

Harold's main contribution to the work of the garden during the war was in hedge-clipping, pleaching his own dear lime trees and as always, weeding. He was an obsessive weeder. "Weeded Spring Garden" continued to be a recur- ring entry in his diaries. In August, 1943, he wrote a vivid essay on weeding for *The Spectator*, his pen dipped in the bitter ink of experience.

"August . . . is the month in which those of us who are clumsy with the shears, who have not those deft ripples of the back-muscles which make the good harvester, are set down, in our few hours of holiday, to scratch and pull and push those horrible invaders from the soil. There is the process known as 'digging them in' which is not only exhausting in itself but which stimulates the weed to recurrence; *tamen usque recurrat*. There is the Dutch hoe, which when the weeds are small or young and the soil loose produces neat and rapid effects, marred only by the difficulty of thereafter collecting and destroying the frail seedlings which have been dislodged. And there is the trug and hand-fork system of weeding, which requires patience but no excessive industry, and by which one can without undue effort clear three square yards in as many hours. I prefer the latter system since it is good for soil and soul alike. Not only are the weeds enucleated, but one's character is improved by doing a dull thing thoroughly. The weed that the spade digs in, the weed that the hoe snaps, are by this slow process taken individually, each little severed stem becomes a case of conscience; to leave it uneradicated is a moral defeat; a sense of achievement is caused when the most brittle tap-root is gouged like a carrot from the earth." He adds that never again will he think the garden-boy slow.

RIGHT
Sissinghurst is essentially a
country garden, with formal
enclosures melting easily
into the wild.

BELOW
Great hedges form the garden's
bones. The Rondel in the
centre of the Rose Garden is
circled by yew.

ABOVE
The Herb Garden is planted
with herbs in great variety.
The marble bowl resting on
three lions was brought back
by the Nicolsons from Cospoli,
Constantinople, in 1914.

LEFT
A rose-covered arch leads to
the Tower Lawn. Thick box
hedges shelter a bed of
eremurus.

"The defensive war which through four long years we have conducted so unsuccessfully against nature has taught us more about gardening than we ever knew before . . . in this matter of weeds we have enormously increased our experience . . . in view of the fierce profligacy of nature, it is a triumph for the gardener if any flowers grow at all."

Vita, too, wrote about their war on weeds, more solemnly, and in verse.

> "So in the gardener's more persistent war
> Where man not always is the conqueror,
> We plodded as we could, and fought
> Permanent enemies, of weed and wing:
> The strangling bindweed and the running strands
> Of crowsfoot, and the suckers of the rose,
> Inordinate thorns that mangle our poor hands;"*

The "enemies of wing" were a plague of wasps which swooped one year on the fruit.

As the war dragged on – the war against the Germans, not the war against nature – the garden did perforce go back. Temporary plants, such as annuals, were finally abandoned. The grass grew knee-high and was scythed and made into hay. Their dear donkey, Abdul, grazed on the Tower Lawn. Brambles and thistles, docks, bindweed and ground elder made their hideous encroachments in spite of the Nicolsons' valiant efforts. The Herb Garden was completely smothered. The wood, to Vita's fury, was invaded by the army, its flower-strewn soil furrowed by tanks. "I feel that I and the lake and the wood are all damaged and spoilt for ever" she wrote in December, 1944. Even so, the trees grew on, the roses bloomed, the vegetables cropped, the irises and lilies scented the air, the cottage garden blazed with colour, the magnolias bore splendid blooms, some narcissus bulbs which they had dug up years ago in Persia flowered for the first time, and at the end of the war Harold was still able to refer to Sissinghurst as "that shrine of quiet and loveliness."

* *The Garden.*

A smaller, but gratifying success was the usefulness of their donkey from Morocco. In 1943 Vita wrote to Harold "Abdul really is justifying his existence now. I met him dragging his little cart full of leaf-mould, and he brings all the pea-boughs home for us too. He does look so tiny and sweet in his cart, and he is so serious and pulls so hard. I gave him a carrot, but he was too pre-occupied to eat it."

It must not be inferred, from such anecdotes as that of the onion-stealers and from Vita's hostile reaction to having the army in the wood, that she was indifferent to the war. On the contrary, she read the newspapers avidly, listened anxiously to the news bulletins, thought much about her absent sons and rushed for their letters. Her physical courage never faltered but her natural melancholy ran deeper than ever, especially after the suicide of her friend Virginia Woolf in 1941.

She sometimes felt that gardening was a trivial occupation in the anguish of Europe and wrote a little apologia in *The New Statesman,* for which she continued to write country articles in the early years of the war, saying "my only excuse can be that the determination to preserve such beauty as remains is also a form of courage." In another article, she defended the cultivation of flowers in wartime with the valid argument that "man cannot live by potatoes and onions alone."

Her poem *The Garden,* begun in 1942, is suffused with *lacrimae rerum,* but her tears were always for small, personal, not large, communal tragedies. It was the impact of violence on the quiet country scene which moved her most, the bomb crater in the cornfield, the killing of a bird.

"Strange little tragedies would strike the land;
　We sadly smiled, when wrath and strength were spent
　Wasted upon the innocent.
　Upon the young green wheat that grew for bread;
　Upon the gardens where with pretty head
　The flowers made their usual summer play;
　Upon the lane, and gaped it to a rent

So that the hay-cart could not pass that way.
So disproportionate, so violent,
So great a force a little thing to slay.
– Those craters in the simple fields of Kent!

It took a ton of iron to kill this lark,
This weightless freeman of the day.
All in its fate was irony. It lay
Tiny among monstrosities of clay,
Small solitary victim of the dark."

Of all the calamities of the war, it was the bombing of
Knole in 1944 which hurt her most. "I mind frightfully,
frightfully, frightfully. I always persuade myself that I have
finally torn Knole out of my heart, and then the moment
anything touches it, every nerve is alive again. I cannot bear
to think of Knole wounded, and I not there to look after it and
be wounded with it. Those filthy Germans! Let us level every
town in Germany to the ground! I shan't care."

Knole was bombed (though not seriously damaged) but
Sissinghurst remained immaculate, preserved, perhaps, by
the intensity with which Vita wished it so. Her passion for
continuity rose above all material difficulties.

"We had just counted a third wave of forty bombers and
fighters roaring past, leaving white streamers like the wake
of ships across the blue. 'Please, madam,' said a quiet voice,
'would you like luncheon out of doors? Then you could
watch the fights better.'"

Vita recorded this little incident in 1940 as though it were
the most natural thing in the world. In the violence of war,
luncheon at Sissinghurst was still served in the garden – and
since bees were kept at the farm, there was honey still for tea.

9

After the War:
Revival and Full Bloom

Sissinghurst was soon to reach the period of its finest flowering. The trees were mature. The hedges had grown to the stature necessary to guard the secrecy of the enclosures. The gardeners came home and scythed and mowed, weeded and clipped, sowed and planted until Sissinghurst was Paradise regained.

John Vass, the head gardener, returned in 1946, and he and his team worked through the garden bit by bit, starting with the Front Courtyard, where the weed-infested turf was dug up and a new lawn sown. The most overgrown enclosure was the Herb Garden, which had to be dug over and planted with early potatoes to clean the ground, before it could be replanted with herbs. It was at this point that the twenty beds were made and planted with the rich variety of herbs one sees today. Copper, the chauffeur, constructed the curious stone seat in the Herb Garden which was dubbed Edward the Confessor's chair.

While the weeding and replanting were going on all over the garden, the moat was cleaned and its fallen bank rebuilt and the lake was dredged. Though it took five years to bring the garden to perfection, it was much restored by 1948, when the rebuilt moat bank was re-turfed, the job being miraculously completed in three hours. Vita reported a "remarkable transformation", the turf arriving in "huge Swiss rolls." Harold replied "the new bank sounds lovely, but I wish we had pricked out 5,000 croci in it before the turf was laid."

In the early years after the war, Vita was still in good health and at her peak both as a plantsman and as a gardening writer. Horticultural honours were showered on her. Visitors came from all over the world to see the garden she had made, and she enjoyed the appreciation of the genuine gardeners. "It was a nice society that came yesterday" she wrote in May, 1948, "very keen gardeners and quite knowledgeable." Soon afterwards came a party from Holland and then a party of archaeologists from Canterbury, both welcome. Parties of foolish clubwomen were less popular. Vita felt that equivalent parties in France or Italy would be more intelligent and better informed.

As for Harold, the garden was an unfailing source of pride, comfort and delight. After a garden tour in England and Scotland they returned to their own Sissinghurst to find "we prefer it to all those we have seen, with the exception of Hidcote."

Harold continued to visit Flower Shows, as he had done all his life, sometimes rashly placing orders which he was not supposed to do on his own.

In June, 1948, they quite absurdly went to the same Flower Show independently and wrote their views to each other the next day, their letters crossing. Their opinions coincided remarkably. Both picked out certain peonies and carnations as the most beautiful plants in the show. (Vita characteristically disapproved of the giant delphiniums. It was "like coming into a hall of peacocks' tails fully spread, but I did not covet them: they are too bogus.") Harold had ordered some of the carnations, and Iceland poppies, too, and had to explain himself. "I felt so sure that you would not be going to the Flower Show that I broke our pact and ordered things on my own ... my justification is that you spend all your money on the garden and I get the pleasure out of it. Thus I like ordering things myself and getting the bills." Harold was always a more generous buyer than Vita, ordering in quantities where Vita usually ordered one of a kind.

The first milestone after the war was the making of the White Garden. The site Vita had first thought of, the place where the Lion Pond had been, was not chosen, for Harold and Vita realized that it was too shady, and the sunny enclosure between the Tower Lawn and the Priest's House, where the Nicolsons had made a rose garden some seventeen years earlier, was chosen instead and planted with a colour scheme of green, grey and white. It was to become one of the most famous gardens in the world and is usually held to be the loveliest part of Sissinghurst. In June, the Rose Garden contests this place, but the White Garden holds its peak far longer, from June to late September. The planting will be fully described in a later chapter, but as a matter of history, the garden was conceived in 1939 and planted in the winter of 1949–50. The first plant to go in was the silvery Willow-leaved Pear, which was moved into the new garden from the Rose Garden, where it had been planted some years earlier. The Rosandic statue was moved from its place outside the dining-room window to stand under the sheltering branches of the pear-tree.

The plants of the White Garden cost exactly £3, for it was stocked from cuttings and roots taken from all over the garden and with lilies grown from seed. The main new purchases were of *Crambe cordifolia* and *Gypsophila* Bristol Fairy. Friends made their contributions, too; for instance, the white weigelas on the garden wall came as cuttings from Hever Castle.

While the White Garden was still being dug and the first plants were going in, Vita described the garden of her mind's eye in an article in the *Observer*.

"I hope you will survey a low sea of grey clumps of foliage, pierced here and there with tall white flowers. I visualize the white trumpets of dozens of Regale lilies, grown three years ago from seed, coming up through the grey of southernwood and artemisia and cotton-lavender, with grey-and-white edging plants such as *Dianthus* Mrs. Sinkins and the silvery mats of *Stachys lanata*, more familiar and so much nicer under its English name of Rabbits' ears or Saviour's Flannel. There will be white pansies, and white peonies, and white irises with their grey leaves . . . at least, I hope there will be all these things. I don't want to boast in advance about my grey, green and white garden. It may be a terrible failure. I wanted only to suggest that such experiments are worth trying, and that you can adapt them to your own taste and your own opportunities.

"All the same, I cannot help hoping that the grey ghostly barn-owl will sweep silently across a pale garden, next summer in the twilight – the pale garden that I am now planting, under the first flakes of snow."

Vita's vision was more than realized. Many more white plants than those in her list soon speared the green ground cover, and smaller white plants crept across the paving. Harold, looking over her shoulder as always, besought her not to be tempted into allowing any coloured flowers to intrude into this subtle scheme. "Although I would welcome a fid or two of anchusa or something else blue among these white and silver objects, I hope you will keep the main colour scheme firm. Otherwise it may all look just like a flower-border anywhere." She did, in the event, keep to the colour scheme strictly.

Another new feature at this period was the Thyme Lawn, made in 1950, just outside the Herb Garden. A bed of hollyhocks had been tried on this spot, but it was too windy a corner for them, and Vita devised instead the tapestry of creeping thymes. Roots of red, purple and white *Thymus serpyllum* were collected from crevices all over the garden, and formed a thick mat within a year.

Throughout Sissinghurst, the range of plants improved and increased in these halcyon years, some chosen from nursery catalogues, some ordered at flower shows, many acquired from private collectors and friends, such as the Aberconways at Bodnant and Sir Frederick Stern at Highdown, for Vita was now moving in the loftiest horticultural circles. The Ingwersens gave some choice alpines to plant in the high beds cut into the old Elizabethan wall. Wherever she went, Vita collected seeds and roots and cuttings, and always travelled with a spongebag and a few potatoes into which she would put cuttings to keep them moist and fresh.

A typical shrub order from Hillier's of Winchester was recorded in the autumn of 1952, when Vita sent for *Nandina domestica, Indigofera pendula, Decaisnea fargesii, Solanum crispum autumnale* Glasnevin, *Buddleia fallowiana alba, Buddleia nivea, Philadelphus microphyllus, Salix fargesii, Coriaria terminalis xanthocarpa,* 2 *Deutzia rosea,* 2 *Deutzia* Pride of Rochester, *Genista variegata, Schizandra grandiflora rubrifolia.*

New moisture-loving plants, like meconopsis and rodgersia, were obtained for the former Lion Pond, which was turned into a sunk garden. New herbaceous plants were ordered to enrich mixed borders. "The Tower Lawn. Yes! Yes! Yes! the pink *Eremurus warei* that I saw at the Maidstone Show. That is the place for it. I have ordered four from G. and A. Clunk, Devon. They flower late, i.e., July. Give them some lime."

The collection of roses, already so magnificent, was added to from new sources. Some were sent over by Constance Spry, a long-standing connoisseur of old roses, from her garden at Winkfield Place, some came from Vita's friend and fellow-gardener, Miss Nancy Lindsay, and many from Miss Hilda Murrell's specialist nursery at Shrewsbury. Miss Murrell first went to Sissinghurst in 1952, to see the roses and to thank Vita for sending her customers, and naturally became firm friends with Vita, for their taste in roses was identical. Harold and Vita later visited her nurseries on their way from Hidcote to Bodnant. Others, again, came from Hilling's of Chobham.

Fortunately, there exist two catalogues marked by Vita with crosses against the roses she particularly liked. When her friend Mrs. Lees-Milne was making her own garden at Rocquebrune, in the South of France, in 1954, Vita sent her a Murrel catalogue with recommendations. There are three crosses each against Charles Mallerin, Ena Harkness, Etoile de Hollande, Lawrence Johnston, Félicité et Perpétue, Gypsy

Boy, William Lobb, Blanc Double de Coubert, and favourable marks, too, for White Wings ("divine"), Fantin Latour, Comtesse du Cayla, Souvenir du Docteur Jamain, Fashion, Masquerade, *Rosa turkestanica* ("a sort of harlequin"), Paul's Lemon Pillar, *Rosa sinica* Anemone, The Garland, Tour de Malakoff, Cardinal de Richelieu, Charles de Mills, Du Maître d'Ecole, *Rosa gallica complicata*, Parfum de l'Hay. One or two roses of brasher colour are condemned as "stockbroker roses."

The other is a 1953 Hilling catalogue which John Vass has preserved. One hundred and seventy roses are marked as being grown at Sissinghurst, and Vass recalls at least twenty-four other varieties not in the catalogue.

Vita's own roses were still grown in a jungle (her own expression), sprawling, intertwining, barely tamed. The whole garden was still planted so that the flowers seemed a spontaneous explosion of nature – and only a gardener can appreciate what artistry is needed to achieve an abundance which is not a mess. Vita and Harold still gave a welcome to impromptu seedlings. One year, the concrete path of the Lime Walk was thick with self-seeded eschscholzias, but the gardeners were not allowed to uproot them. Another year, when the grass of the Moat Walk was still long and rough after the war, a mass of lupins seeded there. When the gardeners came to mow the grass, Vita insisted that they leave a large pool of lupins in the middle of the path. Moss on paths was always encouraged.

Vita still preferred the shrubs and hedges to be but lightly trimmed. The gardeners complained that the hedges were never clipped hard enough to make them solid and that the ladders swayed, but Vita liked them loose and feathery. Once, Vass, without asking permission, trained the sweet briar hedge behind the South Cottage to wires, which made Vita really angry. She said it looked like a sheep pen.

Botanically, the garden was stuffed with interest, for she had applied her considerable intellect to gardening over most of a lifetime and had become a collector on an important scale.

As the range of plants increased, Vita found new ways of using the new plant material. She liked an element of surprise in her planting (as Harold liked it in garden design), and her plant associations were never banal. An artist of her calibre could afford to shock the eye. For instance, the bronze urns from Bagatelle would not be planted with pretty trailing plants, but with fierce, spiky plants or plants of strong, harsh colour. The visitor's first instinct might be to say "how could she do that?". But the sensitive visitor would see after a while that the choice was profoundly right – a true artist's painting rather than a picture postcard.

During most of this period, from 1951 to 1961, Vita kept a garden notebook as methodical as Harold's book on the Spring Garden, but more discursive. In it, she keeps up a running dialogue with herself about her garden plans. It is a foolscap notebook elegantly bound in green cloth and lettered in gold on the cover: "V. SACKVILLE-WEST. THE GARDEN. Garden Notes." Here are full lists, with prices, of plants to order, notes of plants to be moved, increased or scrapped, of cuttings to be taken and seeds to be sown, and, firmly and satisfyingly, beside every entry, in red ink or chalk, is always the word DONE. "Rondel Border. Scrap amadis and replace by *Rosa rubrifolia* from the orchard. Scrap the acanthus that isn't the right one. Plant lots more Hidcote lavender (useful in August.) Remove the Grootendoorst and replace by Sarah van Fleet." All are marked in red chalk, DONE.

Many other entries show what a perfectionist she was, never satisfied with a planting which could be improved, and how mobile the garden was, no corner left to ossify. There is endless moving of plants.

"Move Leonie Lamesch. She swears with *Rosa mundi*. Replant her near Mutabilis and Pinocchio." "Divide and increase the little violet with dark leaves! Get *Ornithogalum nutans*. This might be better for Delos. Untidy leaves. Nice to pick." "Orchard: more daffodils are needed to sweep forward along the main mown path." "Move some of the *P. florindae* seedlings from the Lion Pond to the nuttery or to the foot of the azalea bank where it is damp." "Take out the white thyme from the thyme bed. Replant it in the grey-and-green garden and replace it by as much of the good *red* thyme as we can spare and fill up with purple." "Move Sir Cedric Morris seedlings – they are unworthy, with the exception of the bronze ones I have marked. Replant them in a little group by themselves on top of the North moat wall, remembering that they have not *all* flowered this year, and there may still be something worth preserving among them. Make the little group near *Rosa paulii*. Replace them, because they will leave a blank, by Variegata di Bologna – a flaky rose. Hillier's and Murrell both have it – and another *gallica complicata*. Spring Salonika lilies amongst them?" Always in red ink, firmly, the word DONE.

Vita was not extravagant when ordering plants, but compared prices between one list and another and often ordered quite small quantities of plants which she could increase by propagation. She notes: "14 *Lannesiana erecta* [*Prunus lannesiana*] to line the path across the orchard. No, 14 would be extravagant. We could have them one side only, or we could stagger them."

Varied and exotic are the plants she orders: *Agathea coelestis, Echinops tournefortii, Oxydendron arboreum, Senecio przewalski, Syringa josikaea, Billardiera longiflora, Grevillea rosmarinifolia, Moltkia petraea, Xanthoceras sorbifolium.*

There are other lists in the notebook of plants to be sent to friends, for gardening is a freemasonry, a club in which much business is carried on by barter. "'Seeds of L. centifolium to Patrick Synge." "Lily regale seeds to Mrs. Kelly." "Myrtle cutting for Mrs. Carey." "A root of comfrey Mrs. Youle, Grand Drive, Raynes Park, S.W.20." "To the Hon. Mrs. Fitzroy Maclean, seed of onopordon, root double blue geranium, cutting of white cistus." DONE, DONE, DONE, DONE. Many were the friendly little parcels that went back and forth.

If Vita was in her heyday as a plantsman through this post-war period, she was at her peak as a gardening writer, too. For fourteen years, from 1946 to 1961, she wrote weekly gardening articles for the *Observer* which did more to change the face of English gardening than any other writing since Robinson's *The English Flower Garden*. Concise and informative, but tinged with poetry, they were models of journalism, and their influence on other gardens was incalculable. Families pounced on these articles at the Sunday breakfast table and, consciously or unconsciously, the upper crust of gardeners began to grow things in the Sissinghurst manner.

Thousands of climbing roses were planted at the feet of apple trees all over Britain. Hybrid tea roses were discarded in favour of shrub roses. Cottage plants and scented plants, herbs and green flowers, winter-flowering shrubs and sweet-briar hedges, sink gardens and pond gardens, bulb species and miniature flowers, clumps of lavender and ribbons of violets, wild corners and seedlings sprinkled in the cracks of paving, became commonplace. Many gardeners greatly increased their range of plants, learned Latin names, grew rarer plants than they had attempted before. The Sissinghurst disciples were mostly of an upper social class, for gardening has its social strata like everything else. The suburban gardener preferred a tidier, more regimented sort of garden and the working-class gardener stuck to his vegetables relieved by bedding plants, but it is not the size of a garden which dictates its style. Large or small gardens, country or town gardens can be and often are planted in a cottagey manner. Of the grand gardens of England, only the great landscapes and the formal Italianate gardens remained unaffected by the Sissinghurst influence.

In these years, horticultural responsibilities and honours devolved upon Vita. In 1949 she became a member of the National Trust Gardens Committee and sat on the executive of the Society for the Preservation of Rural Kent, and in 1955 she was awarded the Veitch Memorial Medal by the Royal Horticultural Society "in recognition of her services to horticulture." She was aware of the increasing responsibilities of being "a gardening V.I.P.", had a heavy correspondence (nearly every letter was answered personally), and received visits from garden professionals and experts as well as from amateurs.

The Press began to regard Sissinghurst as a plum subject. The editor of *Gardening Illustrated* asked permission to write an article, which pleased Vita greatly, and the garden was photographed for *Vogue*, but *Picture Post* sent a photographer unheralded, which not unnaturally set Harold in a rage. "A dreadful woman burst in upon us" he wrote. "I am very firm. But Vita with her warm-heartedness is weak. She calls it 'being polite'. Anyhow I refuse to be photographed, and go off and weed. I am weeding away, grunting under a forsythia, when I realise she is behind me with her camera. All she can have photographed was a large grey-flannel bottom."

There was a similar disagreement between Harold and Vita on the subject of a television programme proposed by the B.B.C. Vita was willing, Harold was not, having a prejudice against "exposing my intimate affections to the public gaze." Vita gave way and Sissinghurst was not televised.

Increasingly, paying visitors poured into Sissinghurst, coming in thousands in the course of a summer. Sometimes Vita sat on a bench behind the table – "like a spider watching for prey" says the Vicomte de Noailles – but a kindly spider, for it is said that nobody was ever turned away for arriving after hours. In the afternoons, if she was not behind the table, she would be found working in the garden, as ready as ever to talk to the shillingses and answer questions. In later years, when he had become less active than formerly as a weeder and bulb-planter, Harold could be seen sitting on a chair in the middle of the Lime Walk directing the exertions of his special gardener.

Celebrated as the garden had become, and dearly loved as it was by both the Nicolsons, it never usurped the time they had always given to their writing. "I re-do Chapter XI [of his book *Benjamin Constant*] and finish it. I then clean up my notes etc. I start dividing the primroses in the spring-garden" was a characteristic entry in Harold's diaries. And again: "I have had a really full Sissinghurst day. I write my

review of Samuel Butler. I then write an obituary of Winston
for the *Observer*. I hope to God he isn't going to die. I then
garden for a bit, and write my Overseas Talk for Tuesday.
About 5,000 words in all." On another occasion, he reviewed
a book on Bernard Shaw by C.E.M. Joad, and then relaxed
by going into the Spring Garden and planting white muscari
and *Anemone* Creagh Castle.

Vita's major literary work after the war was *Daughter of
France*, a biography of La Grande Mademoiselle, Duchesse
de Montpensier, who lived from 1627 to 1693. She began the
book in 1947 and finished it ten years later, laying it aside
at intervals to write three novels.

She not only wrote prolifically about gardening; she read
a vast number of gardening books and accumulated a considerable library which is still as she left it in her sitting-room
in the tower. Some of the books were presents from Harold.
As early as 1918 he gave her *My Garden*, by Eden Phillpotts,
and he later gave her the E. A. Bowles trilogy. Of the gardening classics, she read, among others, Robinson, Bowles,
Miss Jekyll, Eleanour Sinclair Rohde, Reginald Farrer,
W. J. Bean and various early books of particular curiosity
or charm such as the Victorian *Rustic Adornments for Homes
of Taste*, by Shirley Hibberd.

There are also many books in the library by modern
authors, some of whom were her friends: books by Patrick
Synge, Lanning Roper, Miles Hadfield, Margery Fish, C. E.
Lucas-Phillips, A. G. L. Hellyer, Will Ingwersen, Roy
Genders. There are also books by the plant hunters, like
Kingdon-Ward and George Forrest and by the great
naturalists like White of Selborne; books about wild flowers
by botanists like Robert Gathorne-Hardy; books on garden
design like Sir George Sitwell's *On the Making of Gardens* and
books on plant nomenclature.

There are specialized books, such as Bowles's *A Handbook
of Crocus and Colchicum; Snowdrops and Snowflakes*, by F. C.
Stern, *The Old Shrub Roses*, by Graham Thomas, and *Old
Garden Roses*, by Edward Bunyard; and monographs on fritillaries, aquatic plants, wild orchids, gentians, primulas,

irises, dianthus. There are books devoted to dry wall gardening, weeds, vineyards, fruit-trees, greenhouse gardening, alpines and even fresh-water aquaria. Most of these were clearly often read and much enjoyed, but numerous others, tucked away on top shelves, seem unread, often sent with the compliments of the author, who doubtless hoped for a mention in the famous column.

In the post-war years, Harold and Vita continued to have minor arguments about garden planning, for he still thought her too impetuous in planting, rushing "just to jab in things which she has left over." But in general, there was harmony and the garden was a mutual joy. They strolled through the wood in spring, walked in the garden by moonlight. They still collected cuttings (poplars again!) on their trips abroad. From time to time they acquired new embellishments for the garden. In 1949 the handsome clock and deep-toned bell which booms over the garden and the weald were put on the tower (Harold had hankered for them for more than ten years); in 1953, five lead urns were bought for the top of the moat wall and in 1954 a dovecote and white doves came for the Orchard. Every Sunday they picked flowers for Harold to take back to London. When they had accepted weekend invitations to go out to lunch they usually regretted it, preferring to stay at Sissinghurst. They revelled in the garden's seclusion.

Harold wrote a definitive description of the garden in October, 1948. "Sissinghurst has a quality of mellowness, of retirement, of un-flaunting dignity, which is just what we wanted to achieve and which in some ways we have achieved by chance. I think it is mainly due to the succession of privacies: the forecourt, the first arch, the main court, the tower arch, the lawn, the orchard. All a series of escapes from the world, giving the impression of cumulative escape."

Another charming reference was in Harold's letter of welcome to Philippa Tennyson-d'Eyncourt who had become engaged to Nigel Nicolson. "You will find Sissinghurst the strangest conglomeration of shapeless buildings that you ever saw, but it is an affectionate house and very mellow and

111

English." Most visitors to Sissinghurst have noticed its oddity as well as its beauty. Jacquetta Hawkes, writing a bread-and-butter letter after a visit in 1951, referred to "the curious and lovely place in which you live."

Another key event in these days of Sissinghurst's zenith was in October, 1959, when two new joint head gardeners were appointed (John Vass had left in 1957) who are still in charge at the time of writing, in 1974. More will be written later of Miss Pamela Schwerdt and Miss Sibylle Kreutzberger, two highly trained gardeners of exceptional quality. Fortunately they were appointed in time to help Vita for the last two and a half years of her life, to learn much from her, to get to know the garden under its creators, so that later they could carry on independently. Another most fortunate arrival in 1959 was that of Miss Ursula Codrington as Vita's secretary, herself a sensitive gardener who became a friend to all the family, and was with Vita when she died.

Both Harold and Vita were perforce less active in the latter years for both were afflicted by ill-health almost simultaneously in 1955 when Harold suffered a minor stroke and Vita, who had for long suffered from arthritis, had a fall on the stairs of the tower and injured her back. Both recovered and continued courageously to write, talk, travel, read and plan the garden with the same enthusiasm as before, and to work in it as best they could. But in 1961, Vita became gravely ill with cancer and in June, 1962, she died, loving her garden to the last day. Though the hand-writing in her Garden Notebook grew shaky towards the end, she still kept the entries going and was still arranging plantings a few months before her death. In the autumn before she died she wrote to Harold: "I've put 400 bulbs in the orchard (fritillaries which you despise, *Narcissus cyclamineus* which you like, *Ornithogalum* which is supposed to naturalise itself but which I have never yet induced to grow, and *Narcissus* 'La Riante'). It seems rather silly, but as Voltaire wisely remarked, *Il faut cultiver notre jardin*. It is really better to have created a *jardin* which gives pleasure to us as well as to many other people, than for me to go and sit down in Trafalgar Square."

Many flowers at Sissinghurst are grown at eye level. *Dimorphotheca ecklonis* fills a sink; *Solanum crispum* Glasnevin covers the wall.

Spring flowers in the Lime Walk: *Anemone appenina, Muscari armeniacum, Erythronium* White Beauty, polyanthus and jonquils.

RIGHT
The Lime Walk in full dress at the climax of spring.

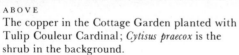

ABOVE
The copper in the Cottage Garden planted with
Tulip Couleur Cardinal; *Cytisus praecox* is the
shrub in the background.

TOP RIGHT
One of many clematis in the garden is the variety
Barbara Jackman.

MIDDLE RIGHT
Clematis Etoile Rose climbs through the shrub
Indigofera potaninnii.

RIGHT
One of Vita's favourite flowers, the spectacular
Cardiocrinum giganteum.

In the following spring, she wrote "The orchard is misty-mauve with *tomasinianus*; *parrotia* flowering as never before. Witch-hazel *arboreus* still out; a few specie crocuses." In early May she achieved a feeble little walk as far as the Spring Garden but she knew that she was very ill and lamented that she would not have the strength to get to the Chelsea Flower Show. On June 5th she died, and a passage from *The Land* was printed on the service-sheet.

> "She walks among the loveliness she made,
> Between the apple-blossom and the water –
> She walks among the patterned pied brocade,
> Each flower her son and every tree her daughter."

10

Vita as a
Practical Gardener

"May I assure the gentleman who writes to me (quite often) from a Priory in Sussex that I am not the armchair, library-fireside gardener he evidently suspects, 'never having performed any single act of gardening' myself, and that for the last forty years of my life I have broken my back, my finger-nails, and sometimes my heart, in the practical pursuit of my favourite occupation?" Vita was somewhat nettled by her peevish correspondent, not surprisingly, since she had regularly planted, pruned, propagated and weeded in the course of her gardening career, and in emergencies had hedge-clipped, hooked and scythed.

How much did she know about down-to-earth gardening? The author thinks her practical knowledge was prodigious. True, she had always had gardening staff and sometimes a head gardener of high quality, particularly in John Vass. Except possibly in the war years she had never needed to plant a hedge or cart manure.

But in all her gardening writing, the authenticity of her experience rings true. She was a highly intelligent woman who read much, observed much, enjoyed handling tools and loved the open air. She was never satisfied with her garden ("beastly garden" she would say when something went wrong), but wanted always to improve it, and when she saw a good method or an imaginative planting in another garden, she tried it at home. Sissinghurst was the scene of many experiments which added to her knowledge.

She was not a labour-saving gardener, but she was a practical one, which is not the same thing. The labour-saving gardener plans for a minimum of upkeep, which may be necessary for his way of life, but Vita did not seek this. Her ideal was to grow a profusion of beautiful plants to give aesthetic pleasure. The tapestry plantings of the Lime Walk and the thyme lawn needed meticulous hand weeding – then let them be meticulously hand weeded. When the men were busy with heavier tasks, she and Harold would weigh in. She spent every afternoon in the garden – working.

Her gardening journalism alone proves that, to put it colloquially, she knew her stuff. Journalism is a great medium for sorting the true coin from the false, for the beady readers of newspapers are only too eager to catch out the writer whose theories do not work. Vita's column in the *Observer* was a unique success because people believed in what she wrote. She recommended a plant, they tried it, it grew. She suggested a garden gadget, they bought it, it worked. The cross gentleman in the Sussex priory was almost alone in his mistrust. When Vita did not know a subject thoroughly, she said so, and was always reluctant to write about town gardens because she had never worked in one. She was practical in that she looked into the thousand problems of a garden thoughtfully and found sensible ways to solve them.

On Soil

Vita was no scientist, but she was practical about soil. She never planted anything without studying its soil needs first. When she was planting alpines she read Farrer: "Farrer says just peat and loam, not dry" she wrote in her Garden Notebook when placing an order for *Gentiana septemfida*; and she looked up other experts for other kinds of plant. "*Colutea arborescens*, the Bladder Senna, ordered from Hillier. A. G. L. Hellyer says poor soil and a hot dry place."

She was well aware of the varying lime requirements of plants, and was careful to warn friends and readers working on alkaline soil if a plant she herself could grow was not lime-tolerant. (Sissinghurst is lime-free, the soil rather heavy; technically it is known as Tunbridge Wells sand, but it is not sandy at all, but is loam on clay.) She knew that *Gentiana acaulis* is a lime-lover, though most gentians are like the autumn-flowering *G. sino-ornata*, which "dies instantly at one distant smell of lime."

One excellent Sackville-West idea for isolating plants in special soil was to collect old broken-down baths, cover the base with clinker for drainage and fill up with the desired mixture. Thus chalk-men could make a peaty place for gentians; clay-men could fill with a light mixture for plants needing good drainage; flinty-men could have a bed of rich loam; hill-men could make a swamp for primulas. Since country junk-shops still have old baths to sell, the idea is as useful today as when she suggested it.

She was a great believer in good cultivation of the soil and thought it the best remedy for diseases such as blackspot. "The orthodox method is spraying with Bordeaux mixture in January and February . . . Some rose-growers also advise a thick mulch of lawn clippings, peat-moss litter, or even sawdust. Others put their faith (such as it is) in rich feeding, on the principle that a healthy, well-nourished plant is more resistant to infection. I must say that I have found this works well. It may sound unscientific, since blackspot is a fungus, and you might imagine that a fungus would establish itself on weak or strong plants equally once it had made up its mind to do so; but I am not a scientific gardener and can judge only by results. The result of some barrow-loads of compost was: no blackspot on some particularly vulnerable roses two summers running."*

She was not a fanatical opponent of sprays or even of weed-

---

* The quotations from Vita's writing in this chapter are either from her unpublished Garden Notebook or from her *Observer* articles, of which a selection was reprinted in *V. Sackville-West's Garden Book*, which is still in print (Michael Joseph).

killers (though she did not like these applied where they would blanket out flower seedlings along with the weeds), but she preferred soil enrichment as a plant protection, especially an autumn top-dressing of compost, leaf-mould, bonemeal or hoof-and-horn, in fact, the slow-acting foods. "Violent stimulants are apt to be dangerous, promoting a soft, quick growth when what the plant needs is a building-up of its underground constitution, to take effect not immediately and dramatically, but in months to come."

Problems of Space

Sissinghurst is a garden of seven acres, but Vita was practical about the problems of a small garden. After all, she had many corners at Sissinghurst to treat as entities. She loved cottage gardens and observed the way they were planted, and she was always impressed by the multitude of flowers in small Mediterranean gardens, where a mere courtyard, balcony or flight of steps is often made rich in plants by the use of pots.

She knew many ways of saving space, getting in far more plants than seemed possible at first sight, and recommended them to other gardeners. Build up a small, flat bed with stones so that you have terraces three stories high and you increase your planting space. (In other words, provide a third dimension). Grow strawberries in tubs and barrels, or alpine plants as an alternative. Use every sort of pot, tub or other container that is suitable and fill it with plants to make the garden lavish. If you have a pocket-handkerchief of garden, do not have a lawn but lay paving instead with spaces to fill with plants so that you have a rug of flowers. "Lakes of **aubrieta, bumps of thrift, mattresses of yellow stone-crop,** hassocks of pinks, rivulets of violets; you see the idea?

"Among these essential and fundamental coverings I should plant small treasures. Shall we say as an axiom that a very small garden should have very small things in it? The picture should fit the frame. I should have lots of little bulbs, all the spring-flowering bulbs; then for the later months I should let the pale blue Camassias grow up and some linarias,

117

both pink and purple, such easy things, sowing themselves in every crevice."

These ideas are now well-known and of course Vita did not invent them all. But she disseminated them widely.

Propagating

Vita loved the various skills of propagation which is one of the reasons why she enjoyed her greenhouses. Her methods varied from the simple business of sowing a ripe apple pip in a flower-pot ("according to the old theory we shake them to hear if the pips rattle, or cut them in half to see if the pips have turned black") to the layering of pinks and shrubs.

"Layering can be done at any time, though autumn and spring are the best. More dependable than cuttings, some proportion of which must always fail save in the most expert hands, layers are almost bound to take root . . . You make a slanting cut in the stem where it is to be inserted into the soil, and then cover it over with earth and hold it down by means of a brick or heavy bit of stone. Best of all is to sink a flower-pot filled with good soil and press the layer into that. By this means, when the time comes for the rooted layer to be separated from the parent plant, usually about a year, the pot can be lifted out of the ground with no disturbance to its occupant, a particularly valuable point in the case of plants which resent disturbance, such as clematis.

"Honeysuckles sometimes layer themselves of their own accord, so avail yourselves of the hint if you want to increase your supply. Azaleas are commonly propagated by layering, but it takes some time to get a plant of decent size. Sometimes it is not practicable to bend a shoot down to meet the ground without snapping it off, and this difficulty may be overcome by raising a pot to the required height, on an old wooden box, for instance, but be careful not to let the pot dry out. This is the easiest method for propagating magnolias, whose side branches generally start rather high up the trunk and are apt to be too brittle to be very flexible."

Few, save E. A. Bowles, have written so lucidly about a garden technique.

Much of Vita's propagating was done with a view to economy. For instance, she always liked to sow seeds of lilies, which can be an expensive plant to keep going in any other way. Unless seed is taken, groups of apparently lusty lilies have a nasty habit of vanishing; lily scales were also saved and grown on. And beds, frames and greenhouses were always filled with cuttings of many plants in due season.

One of Vita's most valuable suggestions was that roses should be propagated from cuttings, so that they would grow on their own roots and not be grafted on to some rose of coarser stock, like *Rosa canina*. Any gardener who has wrestled with rose suckers, getting scratched to pieces in the process, is grateful for a rose which forms a thicket true to itself. Many of the rare roses at Sissinghurst were increased in this way, and Vita knew how to do it.

On Gadgets

Vita liked gadgets, if they were the simple, traditional sort which suited her rustic tastes. "I have found by experience that gadgets, however ingenious and alluring, rarely replace with advantage the old and tried tools . . . Nevertheless there are certain things which one discovers during a life-time of gardening, not gadgets exactly, but helpful hints." She goes on to suggest a huge ball of hop-twine for securing shrubs and roses to their stakes, as being far more enduring than ordinary tarred twine . . . a spool of green string kept in a tin with a hole in the lid, the hole being pierced *outwards* so that the string does not catch in it. She commends a fern-trowel as one of the most useful of all small tools . . . soluble flower-pots (not nearly so widely known when she wrote about them as now) . . . a belt for the gardener to wear with slots for all his tools, knife, string, tin of slug-bait, pencil, tin for seed-collecting, secateurs, trowel. "Each to his choice and need. A belt that Alice's White Knight would have approved. I might take out a patent for it."

How could Vita's crusty correspondent have accused her of being an armchair gardener?

She was also interested in matters of filing, docketting and labelling and tried all sorts of labels to find the simplest and most permanent. She settled in the end for "strips of white plastic which you cut into lengths and fit into a metal holder" (Better labels have been invented since Vita's day).

She dismissed fussy ideas for which she had no time, such as the dipping of cut flowers in tepid, recently boiled water to make them last. "I wonder how many readers of this article are going to go wandering round with a kettle of recently boiled water?" But she would spare any amount of time to achieve a beautiful planting. She found that it was easy to make vague notes of planting plans – "Plant something yellow near the yellow tulips" or "Plant something tall behind the lupins" – and then to forget the meaning of the notes when autumn came and the plants had died down. Instead, she would pick a bunch of flowers *at the time* and stick them in the ground to find which colours and varieties looked best and note them exactly. The picked flowers would be her paints, the flower-beds her canvas. Her colour sense was perhaps her greatest gardening gift.

One Sissinghurst idea which she credited to John Vass was the Sissinghurst way of training vigorous hybrid perpetual roses like Ulrich Brunner and Frau Karl Druschki. "Benders" were made by pushing both ends of some hazel wands into the ground in an arc shape, and the rose would be tied to the benders. It would then break at every joint and flower pro-, fusely at eye level, instead of waving its blooms about high in the air. All the methods of training shrub roses at Sissinghurst are well worth observation. John Vass says that the shrub roses were more heavily pruned than Vita approved. One year, when he had cut them back and trained and tied them she complained that the Rose Garden "looked like a fishing harbour", but he claims that the following summer they were more profuse than ever.

On Pests
Like so many gardeners, especially female ones, Vita was ambivalent about garden pests.

In general, she liked natural rather than chemical resources (preferring stream water to piped water), but she was not bigoted, and approved of sprays for greenfly or fungus diseases. She hated killing things, but knew it could be necessary and summed up the gardener's dilemma perfectly in an article about slugs.

"There is a form of hypocrisy common to nearly all gardeners. It does not affect only the gentle amateur, but has been known to affect even the most hardened professional, who is not, generally speaking, a sentimental or squeamish man. It is the human weakness which, accompanying our determination to rid ourselves of our slugs and snails, makes us reluctant next morning to contemplate the result of our overnight efforts.

"Having enjoyed our own good breakfast, we come out to behold the slimy greenish remains. Big black slugs, four inches long; little black slugs, one inch long; snails exuding their entrails from under their beautiful delicate shells . . . Meta-and-sawdust have done their work only too well. In what agony, during the dark hours, have these miserable members of God's creation perished? . . .

"It is all very painful, unpleasant and even nauseating. What is to be done about it? We must abolish our frail brother with his tender horns, or else sacrifice our seedlings: we have the choice. The seedlings, I think, will win; must win. We must kill their enemies, but, if we are humane in our hearts, we will commit this slaughter with the least distressing offence to our hypocritical selves."

Vita goes on to recommend a reasonably humane anti-slug product. How could that foolish gentleman at the priory have thought that Vita never left her chair by the library fire?

11

The Garden Goes On

Vita was dead. Harold was in declining health. How was the garden to be carried on? Nigel Nicolson had inherited Sissinghurst and its future lay in his hands. The castle and garden had been made between 1930 and 1962 into a unique work of art, a treasure which must on no account be lost, and the obvious solution was to arrange their transfer to the National Trust.

Vita had been sounded on this idea eight years earlier, in 1954, and had rejected it violently. "Never, never, never!" she wrote in her diary. "*Au grand jamais, jamais*. Never, never, never! Not that hard little metal plate at my door! Nigel can do what he likes when I am dead, but so long as I live, no National Trust or any other foreign body shall have my darling. No, no. Over my corpse or my ashes, not otherwise. No, no. I felt myself flush with rage. It is bad enough to have lost my Knole, but they shan't take Sissinghurst from me!" Vita's possessiveness about places – rarely about people – fell little short of hysteria.

It was possessiveness alone that made her so averse to the proposal, not hostility to the Trust, which both she and Harold had always strongly supported. Harold had been vice-chairman of the executive of the National Trust and

Vita had broadcast on its behalf, toured many Trust proper-
ties, and sat on the Trust Gardens Committee. It was clear
to Nigel that the property could not be kept up without some
such support. "My main desire and duty" he wrote* "was to
save what she and my father had created, to preserve in
perpetuity the garden which, together with her books, is the
legacy of her imagination. Few private gardens of this size
could survive in the economic conditions of our time. It was a
choice between its gradual reversion to the fields and cabbage patches from which it had emerged, and the surrender
of the titular ownership to the National Trust. I chose the
second alternative, without hesitation."

Nigel Nicolson therefore asked the Treasury if they would
accept Sissinghurst in part satisfaction of estate duties and
the Treasury agreed, provided the National Trust would
take it over, which they were delighted to do, gaining a
glorious new jewel for their crown. The negotiations were
completed in 1967. Nigel Nicolson helped the finances by
giving an endowment for improvements and upkeep and the
Historic Buildings Council gave an annual grant for several
years until the enterprise could be got on to an even keel.
Today, with income from visitors, rents, the sale of plants
and extras such as teas, Sissinghurst is balancing its budget.

During the "interregnum", between 1962 and 1967,
Nigel Nicolson himself ran the garden and he had considerable assets. The two head gardeners, Pamela Schwerdt and
Sibylle Kreutzberger, both of whom had been trained at the
Waterperry Horticultural School, and were subsequently on
the Waterperry staff, were highly experienced when the time
came for them to direct the garden. By 1974 they headed a
team of six gardeners, the others being George Taylor, who
went to Sissinghurst in 1946, Sidney Neve, who went there
in 1937, Gordon Farris and Mary Digby. Further, Nigel's
wife, Philippa, was taking a great interest in the garden and
she understood its mood particularly well, that strange, per-
vading atmosphere of romance. And various friends of high

* Introduction by Nigel Nicolson to Harold Nicolson's *Diaries and Letters*,
Vol. III.

horticultural standing volunteered to visit and advise, notably Mr. Graham Thomas, Gardens Adviser to the National Trust, and Mr. Lanning Roper. So the garden was well kept up and there were even some developments on the business side, such as an increase in the sale of plants and the opening of a tearoom in the oasthouse of the farm. This was undertaken by members of the Beale family who had lived at the farmhouse since 1936 when a famous Kentish farmer, Captain A. O. R. Beale, took over the tenancy.

The plant stall had been set up in Vita's day on a donkey cart in the external forecourt. Here, characteristic Sissinghurst plants are displayed for sale, many of them plants not easily found elsewhere. On one day there may be *Mimulus glutinosus*, pots of herbs and of abutilon, on another *Cardamine pratensis flore pleno* (double cuckoo flower), the old double clematis *C. viticella elegans plena* and perhaps a selection of fuchsias. All the plants have been grown in the garden or the greenhouses and all are accurately labelled.

When the National Trust took over, the planting of the garden was in excellent shape, but there was much to be done in the way of construction and repair. Some of the architectural parts of the garden were literally giving way, owing in part to the ravages of time, in part to the rapidly increasing number of visitors. In 1961, 13,200 people visited Sissinghurst. In 1967, the number had risen to 47,100. In 1973, it was up to 91,584. (This acceleration is not peculiar to Sissinghurst; garden visiting has become a major recreation in Britain). Therefore, grass paths were beginning to wear down to basic mud; stone paths, laid years before without foundations for the use of a family and their friends, were breaking apart; some flights of steps were proving inadequate. Nature contributed her blows. Some venerable almond trees in the White Garden died under pressure from the enormous climbing roses they were expected to support. The moat had no proper overflow so there were drainage problems in the Herb Garden and Orchard. A substantial programme of architectural repairs had to be undertaken, and it was planned and carried out by a small informal committee

124

consisting of Nigel Nicolson, the head gardeners, Graham
Thomas and other representatives of the Trust.

The first change was in the Rose Garden, where the worn
grass paths were replaced by paths of brick or stone. Soon
after, the Herb Garden was repaved and a new base made of
tiles laid on edge to hold the marble bowl in the centre. This
base was designed by Nigel Nicolson and Graham Thomas.
Then the Cottage Garden paths were relaid, Harold's design
of crazy paving with brick insertions being faithfully followed.

Various ornaments and constructions were put up in the
garden. Harold Nicolson had seen and approved in his life-
time the gazebo in the Orchard designed by the architect,
Mr. Francis Pym, but he died in May, 1968, before it was
finished. This was in 1969, and Harold's sons dedicated it to
their father's memory. In 1970, a slender metal frame was
put up in the White Garden to support the climbing roses
under whose weight the almond trees were dead or dying.
This change had the advantage of letting more light into the
White Garden, where the roses and silver plants were not
getting the sunshine they need. In 1971, the tower steps were
redesigned and by 1972 most of the paths and paved areas
had been re-paved and vital drainage work completed.

In 1971, Nigel Nicolson gave the lake and its adjacent field
to the Trust – they had not been included in the original
transfer – and work began on the drainage and restoration
of the lake and there was some new tree planting in the field.
Currently plans are being made to replace the concrete
paving of the Lime Walk with York stone; when it is finished,
all the paving at Sissinghurst will have been relaid.

Has all this restoring and tidying spoiled the garden? It
has certainly changed it, for the garden has lost some of its
mystery. Sissinghurst was full of flaws, but just as the flaws
of a hand-thrown pot have a charm which a smooth, machine-
made pot can never equal, so were the imperfections of
Sissinghurst utterly delightful. They were part of its intensely
personal character.

But the flaws were unsuited to the new conditions, and
tactful changes were inevitable. Two or three people can

duck under a rose-bush which meets another rose-bush across a path, but a thousand people cannot do so without a bumping of heads. Two or three people can pick their way across a broken piece of crazy paving, but when there is a stream of visitors, somebody is sure to twist an ankle. Sissinghurst had to be restored if the public was to continue to enjoy its beauty.

The important thing is that the restorations have been excellently done. The author can find little which jars in the constructional changes made and some substitutions, such as that of York stone for concrete, can be nothing but an improvement. It must be stressed that the basic plan of the garden is exactly as Harold designed it except for the removal of one or two minor hedges.

The planting is a different matter. A design can be permanent, but planting has to change. Some trees or shrubs will grow old and die, others may outgrow their places, smaller plants need to be rotated, new and better varieties of plants are introduced and should be used, a colour scheme goes stale, a humble plant unexpectedly goes rampageous, a change of climate or drainage affects the plant life, a flower-bed goes sick. (Examples of the last two problems occurred in Vita's life-time. The Nuttery at the end of the Lime Walk, which by 1960 had been underplanted with polyanthus for nearly thirty years, was already showing signs of "primula sickness", from which it still suffers in spite of regular renewal of the plants and generous feeding. If the plants are again unsatisfactory in 1974, the planting may have to be changed; Vita herself would probably have done it sooner. And Vita was saddened by the failure of her beautiful gentian bed in the Orchard, into which lime somehow crept and killed the plants.) Every gardener knows, and Vita and Harold knew, that a static planting scheme is both undesirable and impossible. Every part of a garden must be looked at afresh every season.

The philosophy at Sissinghurst has been to preserve Vita's actual plants for as long as possible, to follow her *style* of planting faithfully, to keep the Sissinghurst colours, the Sissinghurst profusion, the Sissinghurst richness of inter-planting and ground cover, but to change the planting schemes when necessary. The gardeners have been outstand-ingly successful. One section of the garden has even improved in their hands, the ever-troublesome Delos, which has been converted from a rock garden into a shrub garden. (The rocks were used as foundations for the gazebo in the Orchard.) The author's only personal criticism is the treatment of the Irish yews, which she finds insensitive. Vita, who loved their wayward growth, would have shuddered to see them trained into stiff cones, but the gardeners argue that they were neglected for too long and grew too large for their allotted spaces and must be kept in order.

There is a further point on which the gardeners must be congratulated; the standard of cultivation and of plant health throughout the garden is extremely high.

The author visited Sissinghurst towards the end of every month from April to October in 1973, recording the plants and noting the harmonies and crescendoes of each enclosure. This was a normal year climatically, as far as any year can be normal in Britain, so it was a lucky year to have chosen. The spring was rather late and the summer was very dry, but for all that it was a fine year for gardeners all over the country. The author found the garden magically beautiful on every visit, each seasonal enclosure reaching its peak near to its appointed time.

There are two possible ways of describing Sissinghurst, either enclosure by enclosure, or season by season. The author has chosen the second way in the following chapters, because the plan of the garden has emerged already in the telling of the garden's history. Further, a garden calendar is more helpful to the visitor on any given day. Here are the plants and garden pictures to look for in spring, in summer, and in autumn. The permanent plantings will probably remain the same for many years; the minor plantings will change as good gardening decrees.

The visitor who wants to recapture the old feeling of the garden and to enjoy the plants in serene conditions is advised to avoid weekends and Bank Holidays if possible, and to go in mid-week, arriving near the hour of opening.

The White Garden ends in an arch with a view of the weald. The flowers are white *Paeonia suffruticosa* and *Libertia*.

Flame colours in summer: the copper in the Cottage Garden is planted with *Mimulus glutinosus*; *Genista tenera* makes a golden fountain behind the Irish yew.

Flame colours in autumn: a row of *Prunus sargentii* dominates the Moat Walk. *Aster frikartii* Mönch makes a ribbon of mauve flowers at the foot of the moat wall.

12

Sissinghurst in Spring

— When skies are gentle, breezes bland,
When loam that's warm within the hand
Falls friable within the tines,
Sow hollyhocks and columbines.

The Land

In any normal spring the merit of a plan of seasonal enclosures becomes apparent at Sissinghurst in April. Instead
of having patches of spring planting dotted all over the
garden, there is intense concentration on three enclosures:
the Lime Walk (or Spring Garden), the Nuttery and the
Orchard. There may be some delightful early bulbs or
blossom to look for elsewhere, but these three enclosures are
at their peak, and when the peak is passed, the concentration
of flower moves elsewhere.

In May, the whole garden is awake. The finest section is
the Moat Walk, but the Cottage Garden, the Rose Garden,
the White Garden and the Herb Garden are already in dress
rehearsal for their main performance later. The earlier
climbers on the walls are beginning to flower, and the sinks,
troughs and pots are full of graceful small or trailing plants.
The following is a selection of the plants which were in flower
in the Spring of 1973. Most will be in the same places, or
nearby, for years to come, subject to the occasional rotations
which good gardening demands. Naturally, the planting of
the pots will be varied from year to year.

129

APRIL

The **Lime Walk** is in full spring dress. The trees have not yet broken into bud but the borders below are thickly embroidered with thousands of the small flowers and brilliant bulbs of spring. Here are native woodland plants, such as primroses and violets, forget-me-nots and pulmonaria, and other plants which blend naturally with bulbs – *Euphorbia pilosa major* and *E. myrsinites*, dwarf irises, auriculas, polyanthus, *Phlox subulata*, *Viola labradorica*, *V. septentrionalis* and *Violetta* Lady Sackville. The innumerable small bulbs, some of them species, some choice hybrids, include tulips, anemones, fritillaries, narcissi, erythroniums, muscari, scillas, chionodoxa.

The bulbs are of great variety in each genus. The anemones include *A. pulsatilla*, or Pasque flower, *A. nemorosa*, the wild anemone of the English woods, its blue forms, *A.n. allenii* and *A.n. robinsoniana*, scarlet *A. fulgens*, *A. ranunculoides*, and the two starry-flowered blue anemones, *A. blanda* and *A. appenina*.

Fritillaries range from the tall orange *F. imperialis*, or Crown Imperial, to the small violet-blue *F. persica*, and there are *F. pyrenaica* and *F. meleagris*.

Outstanding among many tulips are (in approximate flowering order) *T. kauffmaniana*, *T. greigii* Red Riding Hood, with purple and green striped leaves, *T. praestans*, *T. tarda*, *T. batalinii*. There are early single tulips, like Apricot Beauty, Lily-flowered tulips, such as the claret-coloured Captain Fryatt and yellow Ellen Willmott, varieties of the green-flowered *Tulipa viridiflora*, and some Darwin hybrids.

The narcissi include many small varieties, though there are the taller jonquils to prolong the flowering season. Of the cyclamineus narcissi, there are Peeping Tom, Jenny, Charity May and Beryl, then come the triandrus varieties, then the jonquil hybrids, including the tall and vigorous Tresamble, and last of all the old late Pheasant Eye, with its strong sweet scent.

Many small bulbs and creeping flowers escape from the borders and push their way up through the flagstones of the path: muscari, dwarf irises, thyme, anemones, fritillaries, erythronium, tiny rock narcissi, *Viola labradorica* and occasional tulips.

A large oil jar half way down the walk is brimming with *Clematis macropetala*, the dusky buds just opening to reveal their delicate nodding flowers. The Tuscan lemon pots which flank the walk are planted with forget-me-nots.

· The Lime Walk leads at the east end into the **Nuttery** which was for years planted with polyanthus, though this planting has had to be changed. There are clumps of *Helleborus orientalis* under the trees and in the corner nearest the moat there is a counterpane of *Euphorbia robbiae*, with pale green bracts rising above dark green rosettes of leaves.

The **Orchard** is gay with thousands of narcissi growing in drifts among the apple-trees and Japanese cherries of which two varieties are already in bloom – *Prunus* Tai-haku, a variety introduced from Japan by the Nicolsons' friend, Captain Collingwood Ingram, and the double form of the native gean.

Daffodils are not the only flower in the orchard grass. There are *Anemone appenina*, snakes-head fritillaries and clouds of wild speedwell. The yew hedge which divides the orchard from the South Cottage is enhanced by an unusual recent planting; a ribbon of *Euphorbia robbiae* runs along its base, making a harmony of light and dark green.

Other Plantings to Look for in April

. . . the wide border at the south end of the Tower Lawn has two fine but very different magnolias in bloom, *Magnolia denudata*, with great chalice flowers and the starry-flowered *M. stellata*. They are underplanted with brunnera and hellebores.

. . . in the Rose Garden there are some early clematis (*C. alpina* and *C. macropetala* Markhamii), *Dicentra spectabilis* and (usually at the end of the month) the Virginian cowslip.

. . . there are white wallflowers, tulips, pansies and magnolias in the White Garden.

. . . there are magnolias in Delos.

. . . there are tulips, spurges and pansies in the Cottage

Garden in the tawny and fiery colours characteristic of this enclosure; the central copper is planted with Tulip Couleur Cardinal, which has a blue-green leaf to match the copper.

. . . the first of the shrubs in the Front Courtyard to come out in April are usually *Ribes laurifolium* and the flowering quince, *Chaenomeles* Knap Hill Scarlet.

MAY

The **Moat Walk** is spectacular, for the whole bank dividing the walk from the Nuttery is in flower with azaleas whose scent, almost overpowering in the walk itself, is carried far beyond it on the spring breeze, to excite your senses unexpectedly as you turn a corner or change your path. The sweetest smelling is *Azalea pontica*. The moat wall, which has five lead urns on top, sprouts with ferns and with the purple perennial wallflower known as Mr. Bowles's variety. White wisterias drape the wall (*W. venusta* and *W. sinensis alba*); the acid yellow *Euphorbia niciciana* forms carpets round the buttresses.

The **Cottage Garden** is also in full flower in its special colour range of yellows, flames and reds, cooled off with white and green. The cottage itself is smothered from ground to eaves in late May with one of the most glorious roses in the whole of Sissinghurst, Madame Alfred Carrière, with creamy noisette flowers, and the butter-yellow rose, Lawrence Johnston, clambers up the west corner, and also usually starts to bloom in late May.

The beds in front of the house are filled with blood-red scented wallflowers. The four central beds are thick with columbines – a strong feature at Sissinghurst at this season – and with red, yellow and tawny-coloured herbaceous plants. There are geums, asphodeline, mullein, *Euphorbia polychroma*, *E. griffithii* Fireglow and the primrose-yellow peony, *P. mlokosewitschii* (late April – early May). There are many shrubs in flower in the same colour range: the dark crimson tree peony, *P. delavayi*, which has crossed naturally with the yellow *P. lutea ludlowii*, to produce varieties with bronzish flowers, the lemon-yellow broom, *Cytisus praecox*, and *Berberis linearifolia* Orange King.

Gardeners will notice that such flowers as need staking are supported by peasticks which will become quite invisible as the leaves expand. Alas, even at Sissinghurst, with its own woods, hazel peasticks are becoming hard to obtain.

In all parts of the Cottage Garden, ground cover plants spill from the beds on to the paving. One of the prettiest is the annual poached-egg plant, *Limnanthes douglasii*, a primrose-like flower with yellow petals and white centres. Dwarf irises make little pools among the larger plants. There are brown and yellow pansies.

On the east side of the cottage there is a wide border which should not be missed, for there is always something interesting in flower, and many good foliage plants, such as rodgersia, *Euphorbia pilosa major* and *Helleborus corsicus*. Outstanding now are the columbines and that graceful plant which looks like an outsize Solomon's Seal, *Smilacina racemosa*.

The **Rose Garden** is nowhere near its zenith, but the earliest of the shrub roses are already out: the first rugosas, like Roseraie de l'Hay, Blanc Double de Coubert and *Rosa rugosa alba*, with very large blooms, yellow Frühlingsgold, and some of the rose species – *R. farreri persetosa* and a purplish-pink *Rosa spinosissima* called Single Red. Herbaceous plants, early summer bulbs and ground cover are abundant, some out, others in bud. In the taller ranges there are groups of bearded irises, splashes of columbines, tulips (until mid-May); notable among many smaller flowers are dwarf irises, large, plum-coloured pansies and ajugas. Early clematis flower on trees and walls.

The **White Garden** is not yet the cool oasis it will be in midsummer, but its mood can already be understood. It is a ghostly garden, a Tennysonian garden, where Maud or Mariana might have walked, but never an insipid garden, for the white flowers with which it is exclusively planted are set off by the rich green of box and the fresh greens and silvers of many foliage plants. In flower in late May or early June is a spectacular *Paeonia suffruticosa*; its enormous white flowers, with purple feathering inside the petals and yellow stamens, are some ten inches across. Also out are white columbines, potentilla, pansies, wallflowers, the waving spires of *Eremurus himalaicus, Iris florentina* and *Thalictrum aquilegiifolium album*. Madame Alfred Carrière covers the east face of the Priest's House.

The **Herb Garden** is charming now, its season being almost continuous from May to October. Growing strongly are *Isatis tinctoria* (or woad), parsley, *Santolina chamaecyparissus*, comfrey, Cologne mint, fennel, artemisia, bistort, golden origanum, foxgloves, *Helleborus foetidus*, clary, caraway, chives, curry plant, white and blue borage, *Pulsatilla vulgaris*, *Geranium macrorrhizum*, many thymes, many sages, nepeta, mandrake, dyer's greenweed, tarragon, monarda, pennyroyal, elecampane and angelica. The marble bowl from Cospoli is planted with house leeks and the stone seat is cushioned with chamomile. Some of these plants are in flower, some will flower later, but with most herbs the flower is not a conspicuous feature. It is the foliage and, of course, the scent, which are important.

Other Plantings to Look for in May
. . . in the Front Courtyard, the flowers in the Purple Border are coming into bloom. This is the border along the north side devoted to flowers in shades of mauve, red and purple, blooming now with tulips, pansies, irises, wallflowers, bistort, columbines, the deep purple *Campanula glomerata*, and, at the end of the month or in early June, *Rosa moyesii*. At the opposite end of this courtyard are many aquilegia hybrids, *Rosa willmottiae* and *Viburnum tomentosum mariesii*, trained (which is unusual) flat against the wall.

. . . the earlier clematis are in bloom, especially *C. spooneri* and *C. chrysosoma*, forming heavy curtains in the Tower Lawn Courtyard, where the white *C. spooneri* has *Rosa moyesii* growing through it.

. . . long ribbons of *Viola labradorica* are in flower at the foot of the yew hedges of the Yew Walk.

. . . sinks, troughs and pots should be looked at closely, for they are full of graceful small or trailing plants. The four bronze urns at the entrance are planted with *Helichrysum microphyllum*. A sink in the Front Courtyard has *Euphorbia myrsinites*. The tank in the sunk garden at the south end of the Tower Lawn has that most pathetic of plants, *Dicentra spectabilis*, with poor little bleeding hearts nodding from fragile stalks over cut, feathery leaves.

. . . the Orchard is betwixt and between the daffodils of April and the roses of June, but the apple blossom is out early in the month. Swathes of mown grass are cut through the long grass to make wide paths, and wild flowers are allowed to seed in the long grass, such as cow parsley, cuckoo flower, daisies and speedwell.

13

Sissinghurst in Summer

– June of the iris and the rose
The Rose not English as we fondly think.
Anacreon and Bion sang the rose,
And Rhodes the isle whose very name means rose
Struck roses on her coins.

The Garden

In June, July and August, the concentration of flower moves on. Two enclosures are perfection in June, the Rose Garden and the Cottage Garden, though the latter will blaze even more brightly in July. The roses are not confined to the Rose Garden but flower exuberantly in every enclosure, on walls, in flower-beds and in the orchard grass. There is also some interest in the Front Courtyard, particularly in the Purple Border, which is in full flower in its somewhat sombre way.

July sees the peak of the White Garden. The Cottage Garden is still in ebullient flower. The Herb Garden is at its most aromatic, the Moat Walk has fresh interest and there are many beautiful smaller plantings throughout the garden to catch the perceptive eye. The outstanding flower of July is clematis. Clematis with large open faces and others with little nodding flowers look down from every wall. There are white clematis and red clematis, all the purples and mauves, and the small-flowered yellow species. The other flower of the month is the viola. Violas and pansies of every size and hue are tucked into spare corners and into spaces in the beds.

August is a mixed month. The first two weeks are still summery. There may be a lull after the dazzling flower show of June and July, but the structural features of the garden look magnificent in the strong light – the fine trees, dark hedges and green lawns, the water of the moat, the stone statues and the old brick walls. The Cottage Garden is the best of the enclosures now, but the White Garden is still a delight, and there are interesting plants in most of the borders. The walls of the garden are splashed with the purples and blues of clematis, ceanothus and purple-leaved vines.

The second half of August has a tinge of autumn and will be described, linked with September, in the following chapter.

JUNE

The **Rose Garden** is an explosion of bloom, the shrub roses in the great beds round the Rondel bursting in fountains over pools of herbaceous flowers and foliage plants – Sissinghurst has one of the finest collections of shrub roses, especially old-fashioned roses, in the world. The walls of this garden are laced with climbing roses intertwining with other climbers, especially honeysuckle and clematis – the Elizabethan wall at the north side of the garden makes a particularly mellow background for roses. At its foot is a mixed border called the Long Border planted with roses, shrubs, herbaceous flowers and irises.

The shrub roses in the rose-beds are grouped with an eye to their manner of growth as well as to their colours. The compact gallicas are backed by spraying hybrid musks, the dense rugosas, with their distinctive thick, wrinkled leaves, are grouped together. Generally speaking, the colours are arranged to make harmonies rather than contrasts. Some of the roses are tied to chestnut stakes, three or four to a bush, which are replaced every year or every second year when the roses are retrained. Others are trained over tripods, usually with clematis or honeysuckle twining amongst them. Others are tied to hazel benders, replaced annually, as the hazel must be green and pliant. (The only alternative wood for this purpose is ash.)

The shrub roses to be looked for in the Rose Garden in June include the following, though this list is far from complete – the full catalogue would total some two hundred varieties. Of course, the exact moment of flowering will vary from season to seaon.

The hybrid musks have always been important at Sissinghurst, for in addition to scent and beauty of flower, they are recurrent, a rare virtue among shrub roses. Here are Buff Beauty, with clusters of large double apricot flowers, chinapink Felicia, pink-and-saffron Penelope, coppery pink Cornelia, deep pink Vanity and the pure white Pax.

Among the many gallicas are the famous striped *Rosa mundi* and two almost equally celebrated dark crimson roses, the very dark, very double Cardinal de Richelieu and crimson-velvet Tuscany; and there are Alain Blanchard, *R. gallica complicata*, with large single pink flowers, Charles de Mills, Gypsy Boy, Hippolyte, Francofurtana and Président de Sèze.

Among the bourbons, most of them blessed with beautiful names, are Honorine de Brabant, Madame Pierre Oger, Madame Isaac Perèire, Madame Lauriol de Barny, Coupe d'Hébé and Zephirine Drouhin. Among the damasks are Madame Hardy, whose highly scented white quartered flowers have a green button eye, a Ville de Bruxelles, the truepink Ispahan and *Rosa sancta*, the Holy Rose, first found in Abyssinia, where it is thought to have been taken in the fourth century A.D. by St. Frumentius of Phoenicia.*

Of course there are cabbage roses (*Rosa centifolia*), like Chapeau de Napoléon, Fantin Latour, Juno and Tour de Malakoff. Of moss roses, there are the little purple Nuits de Young, crimson Henri Martin and paper-white Blanche Moreau.

There are rugosas like Vita's favourite Blanc Double de Coubert, Roseraie de l'Hay and *R. rugosa alba*. There are

* See *The Old Shrub Roses*, by Graham Stuart Thomas.

hybrid perpetuals like Ulrich Brunner, Roger Lambelin and Souvenir du Docteur Jamain, with flowers of so dark a red they are almost black. This is the rose which Vita found in an old nursery and restored to cultivation. There are varieties of *Rosa alba* such as Celestial, Queen of Denmark and *R. alba maxima*.

Some of these roses are very old roses, while some are comparatively modern, but all are "old-fashioned" in that they have flowers of traditional rose shape and all are richly scented. Musky smells, lemony smells and luxurious, sensuous smells, particularly from the bourbons and centifolias, send up a steam of fragrance on a June day.

There are also species roses in the Rose Garden; most of them flower early in June and may be spent by the middle of the month. Here are red-stemmed, purple-leaved *Rosa rubrifolia*, *R. farreri persetosa*, the Threepenny-Bit Rose, with small soft pink flowers, *R. villosa* Wolley Dod and the carmine, semi-double *R. californica plena*. (Vita had understood when she planted this that it would be four feet high and was somewhat put out when she found it approaching ten feet).

There are also a few hybrid teas and floribundas, such kinds as blend with old roses – Lilac Charm, Magenta, Ellen Willmott, White Wings and the shrub-like hybrid tea, Mrs. Oakley Fisher, with copper-yellow flowers, which was a favourite with Vita.

Climbing plants on the walls of the Rose Garden add their profusion to the climbing roses. On the wall behind the Long Border are *Ceanothus impressus*, *C. dentatus*, *Solanum jasminoides album*, *Clematis* Nellie Moser, and figs and honeysuckles. On the semi-circular wall at the west end are *Ceanothus austromantanus* and the vigorous honeysuckle, *Lonicera grata*, mixed with clematis and vines.

All the rose-beds are thickly interplanted with a wide variety of plants, from surprisingly tall herbaceous plants to ribbons of little foliage plants running in and out among the roses' feet.

There are clumps of campanulas, tobacco plant, *Geranium psilostemon* and other hardy geraniums, tall delphiniums and foxgloves, *Alchemilla mollis*, catmint, pulmonaria, now in the silvery foliage stage, and Japanese anemones, not yet in flower, but decorative in leaf. Of small plants, there are sweet williams, heliotrope and hundreds of pansies. An unexpected but satisfying foil for the roses is the big-headed purple allium, *A. albopilosum*. A splendidly harsh note is struck by the spiky leaves of irises against the feathery columbines. The planting achieves serenity without being sweet or banal.

The Long Border is a glorious mixture now of roses with shrubs, irises, herbaceous plants, sub-shrubs like Lavender Hidcote Giant, and felty-leaved things like mullein and *Lychnis coronaria*. One of the most graceful shrubs in flower early in the month is *Kolkwitzia amabilis*, smothered with little pink trumpet flowers; one of the most spectacular of the herbaceous plants is *Acanthus spinosus*.

Nearly every gardener who visits the Rose Garden, seeing such a profusion of plants, asks the question "How is it fed?" When the Rose Garden is forked over in the autumn, it is blanketed at the same time with a mulch of spent hops. The azalea bank and most of the borders are mulched with the same substance, which acts as a weed-suppressor as well as a food.

The White Garden has also reached its zenith. The metal frame in the centre is covered with a foam of the prodigious climber, *Rosa longicuspis*, a highly scented Chinese species with clusters of single flowers in June. In the beds nearest to the Bishops' Gate there is a tumble of white-flowered plants – *Crambe cordifolia*, campanulas, delphiniums, white hardy geraniums, galega, *Eremurus himalaicus*, clematis, pansies and Rose Nevada. A few grey-mauve plants creep in, like the deep-belled *Campanula burghaltii*, and there are many silver-leaved flowers and foliage plants – the prickly, metallic onopordon, *Salvia argentea*, artemisia, dimorphotheca, *Helichrysum petiolatum*, *Convolvulus cneorum*, hostas and rue.

At the further end, in a maze-like pattern of small beds enclosed by box hedges are white roses (Iceberg and White Wings), with scattered pools of white turk's-cap lilies, columbines and pulmonaria.

The visitor with a sensitive eye for colour will observe the skill with which the pattern of grey and green foliage plants is woven. The White Garden is not just an arrangement of white flowers planted in a green background. The range of greys, silvers and greens used is wide and each group is planted to harmonize or contrast with its neighbours. Spotted leaves (as of pulmonaria) and striped leaves (as of hostas) make their memorable contribution.

The **Cottage Garden**, also, is superb in June, its red, bronze and flame colours glowing in the intense midsummer light.

The central copper is replanted, when the tulips are over, with orange *Mimulus glutinosus*, and a shallow pottery bowl at the cottage door holds a tripod of sticks with *Thunbergia alata*, or Black-eyed Susan, climbing up them, a graceful plant with orange flowers with dark centres and convolvulus-like leaves.

The beds are planted with a cottage mixture – or rather, a sophisticated cottage mixture, for all the varieties are choice and some are rare. Here are columbines, helianthemum, scarlet snapdragons, mulleins, bronze and gold pansies, oenothera, day lilies, potentillas, nasturtiums, achilleas, thalictrum, *Anthemis* Grallach Gold and many more. One of the rarer plants is the perennial trailing *Tropaeolum polyphyllum*, with blue-green foliage.

The shrubs circling this garden are also in golden colours, such as *Hypericum elatum* Elstead and the golden and green-leaved *Elaeagnus pungens maculata*. The small-flowered scarlet nasturtium, *Tropaeolum speciosum*, weaves in and out of a yew hedge and among the central Irish yews.

The **Front Courtyard** should be visited now for its Purple Border, in a colour range of purples, mauves and dusky reds. The rose species, *Rosa moyesii*, is in flower early in the month. Purple-flowered herbaceous plants include *Stachys macrantha*, *Geranium pratense caeruleum plenum*, *G. psilostemon*, *Nepeta sibiricum*, galega, various salvias, the handsome giant cardoon, *Cynara cardunculus*, the dark purple delphinium Black Knight,

141

the imperial purple *Campanula glomerata*, *Thalictrum aqui-legiifolium*, *Clematis durandii* and *Baptisia australis*, an uncommon plant with blue pea flowers. Patches of heliotrope and violas act as ground cover. The intense blue clematis Lord Nevill blooms on the wall.

Other climbers in this courtyard at this season are *Ceanothus* Southmead, *Solanum crispum* Glasnevin, *Hydrangea petiolaris* and *Actinidia kolomikta*, with variegated leaves of bright pink, white and green.

Throughout Sissinghurst, many climbing roses are in flower in June, from the entrance to the moat.

On the outside of the castle there are Meg, with thick clusters of coral flowers, carmine Madame Grégoire Staechelin, Albertine and Gardenia. On the inside, one of Sissinghurst's most famous roses, Allen Chandler, curtains the archway, the old buff noisette rose, Gloire de Dijon, Mermaid, Meg and Blossomtime clamber up the walls. Albertine scrambles up the tower itself on both the west side and the east. In the Tower Lawn Courtyard there are New Dawn and Paul's Lemon Pillar and the double yellow rambler rose, Emily Gray, grows over the Bishops' Gate.

A point of interest to gardeners is that many of the climbing roses and other climbing plants growing in narrow beds near the castle walls, whose feeding roots would be buried under paths or turf, are fed with foliar feed.

The climbing roses in the Orchard reach their peak in June, some still climbing up old apple-trees, some in crinolines at the feet of the trees, some trained up tripods. Amethyste and Auguste Gervais climb up the tree behind the cottage. Another climber in the orchard is *Rosa filipes* Kiftsgate. There are thickets of roses in the grass, especially specie roses – *Rosa multiflora*, *R. omeiensis pteracantha*, with blood-red thorns, *R. rugosa hollandica* (a large group near the dovecote), and the single pink *R. virginiana*. In a bed at the west end of the Orchard is a thicket of the purple-red *Rosa gallica* Sissinghurst Castle, the rose which the Nicolsons found in the garden in 1930.

Round the altar from Shanganagh there is a thick belt of

the Scotch rose, Irish Rich Marbled, with blush-pink flowers. This rose has shiny black fruits like blackcurrants later on.

Other Plantings to Look for in June

. . . Many pots of tender flowers have been put out now that the frosts are past. Pots of yellow *Abutilon hybridum* stand on the curved terrace overlooking the Moat Walk, known as Sissinghurst Crescent. The acacias round the crescent are the survivors of five planted in 1932.

. . . a small, imaginative planting in the Rose Garden is of *Lamium galeobdolon*, or archangel, shrouding the feet of a small classic statue at the east end. The yellow flowers are over, but the lush green leaves variegated with silver gleam against the stone.

. . . in the sunk garden at the south end of the Tower Lawn courtyard the pure blue poppy, *Meconopsis grandis*, is in flower. *Convolvulus mauritanicus*, with satiny purplish-blue flowers, grows here in pots. The white abutilon, Boule de Neige, is in flower nearby.

JULY — EARLY AUGUST

The **Cottage Garden** glows with its own rich mixture of sunset colours. Many of the June plants are still in flower, but the columbines have been succeeded by hypericums, scarlet dahlias and red hot pokers. There are montbretia, anthemis, lilies, achilleas, pale yellow and red nasturtiums, orange potentillas. The beds in front of the house are planted with Venidio-Arctotis. As always, the shaping of the plant groups is as imaginatively treated as the colour combinations; for instance, the spiky leaves of montbretia contrast with the feathery leaves of achillea.

Regular deadheading and trimming of plants is particularly important in this enclosure, where the succession is prolonged for three months or more. Some plants, notably the columbines, are trimmed hard so that the foliage may come again.

Late in July, there is a new wave of orange and yellow plants. The mimulus continues as the centre-point; in the

143

beds round it are the five-foot high *Euphorbia sikkimensis*, the Mexican *Tithonia rotundifolia* Torch, a plant like a giant zinnia, more dahlias, day lilies and tiger lilies, the scarlet *Lobelia cardinalis*, whose dark leaves are almost black, and the spectacular tall red salvia, *S. fulgens*. Yellow-leaved plants, like the yellow form of *Helichrysum petiolatum*, sprawl from the beds on to the paths.

The White Garden is at its best now. The first flush of roses is over (there will be a second flush later), but white phlox, nigella, delphiniums, mallow, hardy geraniums, potentilla and *Hydrangea arborescens grandiflora* fill the maze of beds. There are some tall, exciting bulbous plants – the dominating *Cardiocrinum giganteum*, *Lilium regale* and *Galtonia candicans*. Silvery plants include artemisia, *Stachys lanata* and *Helichrysum microphyllum*. In late July or early August, the nicotianas come on, the giant scented *N. sylvestris* and *N.* Lime Green. The scent of box is glorious on a sunny day.

The Herb Garden is appealing now to those who have nostalgic memories of dry, aromatic places like the maquis country of Corsica or the thyme-clothed mountains of Greece, for the herbs are at their peak. Some of them, best known for their scent or foliage, are showing unexpectedly interesting flowers. The shoo fly plant (*Nicandra physaloides*) is seen to have blue trumpet flowers, the clary is bright with pink and purple bracts, blue borage, yellow fennel, blue succory, pink hyssop, add their colour.

The **Moat Walk** has plants to enjoy, though the azaleas are long over. Groups of lilies have grown up between the shrubs and there are drifts of euphorbias and an orange-scented ground-cover plant, *Houttuynia cordata*. The moat wall is delightful. Fountains of small-flowered clematis spray over the wall (*Clematis viticella rubra* and *C. v. alba luxurians*, its white sepals tipped with green), and a long ribbon of *Aster frikartii* Mönch is planted at the base of the wall stretching down to the moat. This superb tall aster, of mauve-blue with a big yellow eye, stays in flower for two months or more.

The **Lime Walk**, planted for spring, is bare of flowers, but the limes themselves form a green colonnade. (The limes, alas, may have to be replaced within the next few years). The hornbeam hedges behind are laced with *Tropaeolum speciosum*.

In every part of Sissinghurst, there are beautiful clematis. In the Front Courtyard, the wall behind the Purple Border carries some fourteen different varieties among which are Etoile Violette, Abundance, *C. viticella rubra*, Victoria, Ville de Lyons, Star of India, Ernest Markham and *C. jouiniana praecox*. In the Rose Garden, Perle d'Azur covers the semi-circular wall, intertwined with the dark-leaved vine, *Vitis vinifera purpurea*; a petunia-red clematis called Twilight climbs up a winter-flowering cherry-tree nearby. By the old window in the Rose Garden wall there is *Clematis* Gravetye Beauty and opposite *C. jackmanii* grows up a tripod and *C. eriostemon* clambers over roses. Clematis overlooking the Tower Lawn include a scarce texensis hybrid called Etoile Rose, with nodding pink bells, which continues into autumn.

Other Plantings to Look for in July and Early August
. . . the pots, urns and troughs have been replenished and should be looked at closely. (Most carry labels). The urns at the entrance hold *Helichrysum microphyllum*, those on the tower steps *Artemisia schmidtii nana*. A copper urn near these steps is twined round with *Clematis viticella elegans plena*, an old-fashioned reddish-purple double variety. A very dark purple heliotrope, *H.* Marina, can usually be found in some of the garden pots, and pansies in others.

. . . *Alstroemeria* Ligtu hybrids can be seen in the Tower Lawn flowerbeds and sunk garden. Some exotic tigridias grow through foliage plants in the same enclosure.

. . . there are still some good plants in the Rose Garden. There are handsome *Eryngium giganteum* (sometimes called Miss Willmott's Ghost), a number of alliums, large groups of *Geranium wallichianum* Buxton's Blue, and pools of ground cover.

. . . there are some interesting grasses in various parts of the garden. In the Long Border of the Rose Garden there is *Pennisetum villosum*, a tall grey-green grass from Abyssinia blossoming with pussy-cats' tails. In the White Garden there are the stripey *Phalaris arundinacea picta*, or Gardener's Garters; *Millium effusum aureum*, or Mr. Bowles's Golden Grass; and *Elymus arenarius*, or Lyme Grass.

14

Sissinghurst in Autumn

– Gentleman robin brown as snuff
With spindle legs and bright round eye
Shall be your autumn company.

The Land

Autumn is a variable season in every garden. A sharp early frost may knock down plants which would otherwise flower into November, and the autumn colouring of leaves is an erratic phenomenon. However, the weather pattern in Britain seems to have changed in recent years to give us dry, fine autumns, making September and October two of the best months of the garden year.

At Sissinghurst, the turn of the year begins in mid-August, when many leaves turn colour, there are an abundance of fruits and berries and a mass of autumn-flowering bulbs. The bulbs are particularly good in the Orchard, the fruits in the Rose Garden, the leaves in the Moat Walk. The Cottage Garden is the best of the enclosures for flowers, but the White Garden still blooms. Walls everywhere are splashed with the purples and blues of clematis, ceanothus and purple-leaved vines, and with yellow clematis species.

LATE AUGUST – SEPTEMBER
The **Orchard** has its best moment since the spring, with masses of bulbs in the mown grass. There are great drifts of

colchicums, starting with *C. autumnale* and ending with *C. speciosum* and *C. album*. There are also a few autumn crocuses and groups of *Cyclamen neapolitanum* under the rose wigwams. One of the thickets of roses – *Rosa virginiana* – has coloured to yellow and amber. A bush of purplish *Cotinus coggygria* is underplanted with *Polygonum vaccinifolium*, of which the leaves turn scarlet.

The **Rose Garden** has a renaissance now, for some of the roses have a second flush and there are some splendid hips. Roses with recurring flowers include Ulrich Brunner, Roseraie de l'Hay, the pink rambler Gerbe Rose and the bourbon Champion of the World. *R. rugosa alba* is bunched with enormous hips, *R. rubrifolia* with little red ones, *R. villosa pomifera* has round hips and the hips of the rambler Scarlet Fire are conspicuous on the wall.

There are some good associations of late summer plants. *Sedum* Autumn Joy is grouped with *Pennisetum villosum* and *R. rubrifolia*; *Hydrangea villosa* billows above a clump of acanthus. A purple clematis wanders over tall, stiff yuccas. Inky viticella clematis twine through shrub roses. A fine autumn shrub in flower is *Caryopteris clandonensis*, with clusters of blue flowers. A large bushy salvia is out, *S. uliginosa*, with intense blue flowers. There are clumps of *Aster frikartii*, the Japanese anemones are at their best, and there is a strange plant in the Long Border, *Dierama pulcherrimum*, otherwise called Wand Flower or Angels' Fishing Rods, with feathery carmine heads dangling at the end of long drooping stems.

Little rugs of ajuga edge stone paths and ferns spring from the corners of steps.

The **Moat Walk** glows with autumn colour. The azaleas on the bank turn golden, the line of *Prunus sargentii* across the moat wall flames with yellow and crimson leaves, always among the first trees to colour. A graceful perennial plant in the azalea bank is *Gentiana asclepiadea*, with deep blue gentian flowers on arching stems. The blue ribbon of *Aster frikartii* at the foot of the moat wall is as bright as ever; the pots of yellow abutilon continue to flower on the steps.

The **Cottage Garden** is still in flower with dahlias,

nasturtiums, red hot poker and other summer plants happy to linger until the frosts.

The **White Garden**, too, has hardly faltered since June. The rose Iceberg has a second flush of flowers as strong as the first. The nicotianas are abundant. New arrivals are white colchicums, the graceful spider flower, *Cleome* Helen Campbell, and the bell-flowered climber, *Cobaea scandens*. The white flowers of *Hosta plantaginea* are out, the huge pleated leaves of *Melianthus major* have grown five feet tall.

The **Front Courtyard** sees a revival of the Purple Border. The wall at the back is netted with clematis, and with the purple-leaved vine at its best. In the border there are *Rosa moyesii*, richly covered with curious hips, *Cotinus coggygria* (pruned hard in spring so that the foliage is as dark as possible), and many smaller plants: a charming lilac-pink monarda called Beauty of Cobham, *Aster frikartii*, dahlias, *Salvia horminum*, Michaelmas daisies and *Eryngium tripartitum*.

On the walls of this courtyard are some fine *Cobaea scandens*, both purple and white.

Other Plantings to Look for in late August and September

. . . Delos, the difficult, windy corner near the Priest's House, is an area which has been much improved and should be visited in late summer. There are some small trees and shrubs with autumn ground cover. Underneath the strawberry tree (*Arbutus unedo*) are *Cyclamen neapolitanum* and two gentians, *G. macaulayi* and *G. sino-ornata*. There are hydrangeas and hebes underplanted with *Polygonum amplexicaule* and *Liriope muscari*, which look like grape hyacinths. Near the house are clematis and the sapphire blue salvia, *S. patens*.

. . . two *Parrotia persica* at the side of the South Cottage are in flaming colour.

In winter, the garden is closed to the public while repairs on the castle and garden are carried out, the turf is restored and the planting generally replenished. For those who live or work at Sissinghurst, there is much winter beauty in the garden. The winter-flowering trees and shrubs which Vita loved so much abound, and in mild weather the earth blooms with winter irises, hellebores and little bulbs, many of which carry on into April, when the visiting season starts anew.

Vita herself wrote cheerfully of the close of autumn in *The Land* and accomplished no mean linguistic feat in working Latin plant names into the metres of *The Garden*. Some of her verses on the garden in winter appropriately close this book.

From *The Land*:
>Then may you shoulder spade and hoe
>And heavy-booted homeward go,
>For no new flowers shall be born
>Save hellebore on Christmas morn,
>And bare gold jasmine on the wall,
>And violets, and soon the small
>Blue netted iris, like a cry
>Startling the sloth of February.

From *The Garden*:
>Still may you with your frozen fingers cut
>Treasures of Winter, if you planted well;
>The Winter-sweet against a sheltering wall,
>Waxen, Chinese and drooping bell;
>Strange in its colour, almond in its smell;
>And the Witch-hazel, *Hamamelis mollis*,
>That comes before its leaf on naked bough,
>Torn ribbons frayed, of yellow and maroon,
>And sharp of scent in frosty English air . . .

>Gardener, if you listen, listen well:
>Plant for your winter pleasure, when the months
>Dishearten; plant to find a fragile note
>Touched from the brittle violin of frost.

General Index

151

Plant Index

155